TO MANUEL, CH
BER

ACKNOWLEDGMENTS

No story is complete without punctuation marks, and I am so thankful for all of the people who have punctuated my story. All of them have helped advance my story, giving it clarity and meaning: There is Brian Kagan, who, with his creative and loving brilliance, encouraged me to ink my story; and Melissa Holtrop, who, with her unwavering commitment to excellence and administrative genius, has helped me advance the mission of Ink International; and Dr. Craig Ott, who, with his wise counsel, gave me more confidence to explore this new chapter in my life; and Mark Dennis, who, with his loving support and encouragement, allowed me to ventilate my gifts in Evanston and beyond, helping me come into my own; and, last but not least, my dear wife, Alice, who, since we met years ago, has been right by my side, cheering me on, and helping me to become who I was created to be. As my first editor, my champion, my advisor, and my very best friend, she has taught me what true love really is. For all of them I am so grateful.

Prologue

For years, I have been telling my story to audiences, but those presentations were always incomplete. Incomplete because time constraints, attention spans, and propriety all limited me from telling a more complete story.

However, while sharing those truncated versions of my journey with live audiences, I occasionally found myself becoming very emotional during parts of my presentation that surprised even me. Sometimes I would shed a tear, not just about what I was sharing with the audiences at the moment, but also about something else that I did not quite understand. I began to sense that there was a whole lot of something deep down inside me that was yearning to be freed.

So after my presentations were over, and after the audiences had filed out of the venues, I often went back to my hotel rooms, and sat in complete silence. In silence, tried to understand what it was inside me that wanted to be freed. In silence, I reflected upon my journey in more detail, and sometimes I wept. But when the tears dried, and I composed myself, I somehow felt better. There was something about me reflecting on my own journey that was liberating me. My story wanted to be free.

So I began to write, and through several years and tears of sitting in reflective silence, listening to my story try to express itself in the depths of my being, my mind and pen struggled, like a faithful interpreter, to find words that would do justice to the emotions and experiences that have shaped me. My head and hands strained to be neutral servants of the story that is told in these pages.

To be quite frank, I have hesitated to share what has been written in these pages with anyone else. Initially, my goal was just to get the story out, to let it breath, to let it be free. However, in the process of me freeing it, I felt something strange happening- it was freeing me. In the process of me liberating my story, my story was liberating me. Once I finished getting it all out, I felt a little bit of closure. While my story is still incomplete (because I'm still living it), the story told in these pages has really helped to heal some of my hurts, sooth some of my sorrows, and turn some of my griefs into glad hosannas.

Consequently, I began wondering if I needed to share this more complete story with a wider audience. I thought about all the people in the world who might be crying themselves to sleep at night, in need of hope. I thought about those who believe they have no future they can call their own. I thought about those who are being smothered by anger and suffocated by despair. The fact that you are holding this book reveals my response.

In a very real sense, then, it is very likely a miracle that you are even reading this book. First, because of the reasons I just shared with you; and, second, and most importantly, because this book probably should not have been written. You see, statistically, because of the circumstances I share in this book, I should probably be locked up in a cage right now, or a laid up in a coffin, right now. However, by a string of very special events and rather improbable encounters, I am here.

It is from this place, and for these reasons, that I am now compelled to share my story with you. I'm convinced that in the right hands, at the right time, this story might open someone's eyes, renew someone's hope, or even change someone's life. I hope that someone is you.

-Manny Scott

ALL OF THE PEOPLE MENTIONED IN THIS BOOK ARE REAL; MOST OF THEIR NAMES HAVE BEEN CHANGED TO PROTECT THEIR IDENTITIES.

1

It was a place you couldn't really find in the big city. You had to lay eyes on it; you had to touch it, smell it, be there, to get it. In the northeastern corner of Colorado, a hundred and twenty-eight miles from Denver, was a sleepy town wreathed by fields and farms, where life was perfect. It was my home. It was a place where the annual county fair, with its livestock and quilts and corn dogs and snow cones reminded you of why family and community are what matter most. It was a place where the sun sat with you awhile as you rested on bales of hay. So whenever I pause and ponder the first five years of my life, the people and places of Sterling, Colorado are lovingly breathed upon my remembrance.

One of those people who made life perfect was my grandma. She lived in an old, small, light-blue house that sat on the corner of a quiet street. Whenever you walked through her elderly screen door, she would greet her grandchildren with a warm hug and a welcoming smile. When I walked in, she would look at me with her smiling eyes, and say so sweetly, "Hola, mijo mio. How's grandma's boy?"

"Fine," I would say, as I melted into her soft, pillowy embrace. Gram would squeeze me and press her peach-fuzzed cheeks against mine, and kiss me on the cheek, leaving on me a smudge of her rouged red lipstick. She would then look down at me through her rectangular glasses which had broad black rims that covered up her plucked and penciled eyebrows, and, with her thumb or a wet napkin, rub the lipstick off my face. Behind Gram's glasses and smile were deep, brown eyes, clothed with age and filled with grandmotherly love.

Gram had within her the beautiful and rich traditions of both Mexico and Texas. Her mother, my great-grandmother Maria Guevara, immigrated to Texas from Mexico; and, her father, my great-grandfather, whose name was Valentin Guevara, was born and raised in Texas. They raised my grandmother in the San Antonio area, so when Gram spoke English, it was wonderfully textured with a thick Spanish accent.

Gram was also an amazing cook, and we never wanted to miss one of her meals. In Sterling, which had just over eleven-thousand people, with ninety-percent of them being Caucasian, grandma was hands-down the best chef of Mexican cuisine in town. That was her thing. Following a tradition that her foremothers passed down to her from Mexico, grandma rose before the sun every weekday morning to make burritos so she could sell them to the hard-working folks around town.

Whenever you were near her kitchen, the aroma of her authentic Mexican home-made flour tortillas, loaded with moistened chicken, or beef, or pork, bathed in her specially made chiles and sauces, which all melded together into the perfect burrito- whenever you were graced with a whiff of *that*, you leaned into it with mouthwatering delight. If you were blessed with a taste of *that*, your eyes rolled back into your head, and your soul gave thanks.

Then there were her home-made desserts, which came straight from her heart: her pumpkin pie with crust that melted in your mouth like warm, cinnamon butter; and the lemon meringue pie, frothed with whipped cream; and the cheesecake! Oh, on most days, grandma's cooking made whatever was wrong in the world, right, and whatever was right, almost perfect! Almost.

Then there were my brothers Juan and Jose, non-identical twins, who were five years older than I was. My mom birthed them when she was seventeen years old, so they had already matured a little more than most kids their age. They had a special bond, the two of them. Juan was only a minute older than Jose, and he often used his serendipitous seniority as leverage to settle their arguments. He would joke, "Bud, I'm one year older than you, and don't you forget it!"

Then there was Mara, my female cousin who was about a two years older than I was. She was tough, had a smart mouth and the gift of sarcasm- although you didn't think it was quite a gift when she directed it toward you.

And there was Beto, my cousin who was about a year older than me. He wanted to be like Juan and Jose, so although they were 4 years his senior, he, like my brothers, was always a little more advanced than the other kids in the neighborhood. I spent most of my time hanging out with my brothers, Beto, and Mara.

One day, near the end of the summer of 1982, Juan, Jose, Mara, Beto, and I were finishing up one of Gram's sumptuous meals. Juan pushed himself back from the table, stood up, and walked toward grandma's rickety screen door, and on his way out the door he asked, "You guys ready?" We couldn't wait! Even though I needed to use the restroom, we all popped up from the table and ran out the front door to a small tree in front of grandma's house, where a small donkey piñata was hanging. Knees flapping, and tightened sphincter, I could feel the pressure within me slowly rising. But I didn't want to miss out on the festivities.

Mara, with her usual pushy self, looked at Juan and declared, "Me first. Me first. I get to go first."

"Nuh uh," Beto, interrupted. "I get to go first. You always go first, ugly."

With a furrowed brow, Mara crossed her arms, and gave Beto a look of death. "No I don't, Beto! *You're* ugly!"

Jose settled it by having everyone put their feet in a circle. Jose started the process of elimination: "Innie-minnie-miney-moe-catch-a-nigger-by-his-toe. If-he-hollars-let-him-go. Innie-minnie-miney-moe. My-momma-told-me-to-pick-the-best-one-and-you-are-not-it." Whosever shoe got tapped on the final "it" was eliminated from the circle. That was the usual way the kids in Sterling used to determine who was going to go first, or be "it," if we were playing tag or some other game. On that day, I was the last person in the circle, so I got to go first. The treats waiting to be freed from the belly of that piñata made me giddy, so I jumped up and squealed with delight. Mara and Beto didn't share my excitement. I closed my eyes and began dancing. I couldn't help it!

Juan walked toward me with a blindfold in his hand. "Stand still, bud. We gotta blindfold you."

He wrapped the blindfold tightly around my head, but not so tight that I couldn't sneak a peek through the small opening. "Can you see, bud?" he asked.

"Nope," I replied.

Laughing, he pulled up the blindfold a little more, "You think you're smooth, bud."

Once he was satisfied, Jose hollered, "everyone back up unless you want to get your teeth knocked out."

Jose spun me around, while everyone counted to ten in unison. "One...two...three...four...five...six..." At seven, I began to lose my bearing. At ten, I could barely stand. I could hear people laughing at me. Jose grabbed my shoulders, stopping my spin, and faced me toward the piñata. Then he handed me a big tree branch.

"Now go, Eeto," a nickname that he and Juan gave me. It was short for "Manuelito," or "little Manuel" in Spanish. I leaned back and gave it my all. Swoosh! I missed, but I kept swinging, and missing. I stumbled, but Jose grabbed me by the shoulders and positioned me near the piñata again, resetting me. With each miss, the crowd moaned; with each hit, they cheered. "Get it, Lito!" I swung and missed. "Hit it, Lito!"

I swung again. Bingo! They roared.

They were trying to guide me, "To the left." I stepped to the left and gave it my all.

"No, the other left!" Someone else who had had one too many Coronas slurred, "knock the crap out of it, Lito!" Everyone laughed.

I was getting desperate. Looking like a drunk in a fight, I kept swinging. Whop!

"Yeah!!!" They screamed. I punctured the piñata. A few pieces of candy had been knocked loose, but not enough to end the game. So Jose warned everyone, "not yet! Back up! Back up! You're gonna get hit!"

Everyone else got a turn to swing, knocking a little more out of the piñata each time. On my next turn, I whacked it, it busted open, and I heard the ruckus of everyone scampering for candy. I snatched off my blindfold, dropped to my knees, and started snatching as much candy as I could hold in my hands. I felt like I had won the lottery.

My cousin, Beto, high-fived me while chewing on some of the gum he grabbed, "good job, bud." The kool-aid smile on my face said it all. Life was perfect.

I sat down at a little table in front of the house, and I began devouring my candy with carnivorous interest, all while trying not to pee my pants. I couldn't hold it any longer. I swung open the rickety screen door, sprinted through the empty living room, into the bathroom, and slammed the door. As I took care of business, my head went back, and a shiver went through my body. That was a close call. A very close call.

While relieving myself, I heard the intense, muffled voices of my parents through the bathroom wall. In order to eavesdrop, I grabbed a clear glass off the bathroom sink and put it quietly against the wall, just like my mom had taught me. I held my breath, and tried to listen more closely to their argument.

"Don't lie to me, Rose," dad said.

Clearing her throat, mom said, "I'm not, lying."

Unconvinced, he pressed her, "are you sure, Rose?"

"Yes, why would I lie to you," mom assured.

I stood there, still, with the lights off.

"Why don't you just tell me the truth, Rose? He can't be," dad insisted.

Her voice got quieter and shakier. "I'm not going to keep fighting with you about this. I don't know what else you want me to tell you."

"Just tell me the truth, Rose," dad pleaded.

Then there was silence. Neither one of them said anything.

After what seemed like an eternity, I gently pulled the glass away from the wall, and like a mouse, began tiptoeing out of the bathroom. But the stupid door hinges squeaked. "Crap!" I cringed. An empty feeling rested in the pit of my stomach, because I was sure someone had heard me. I stood as still as a statue, trying not to breath, with my heart beating in my throat.

I peeked out the door, to the left. It was clear, so I started to creep by, but there they were, staring straight at me. When they saw that it was me, their postures stiffened. I gulped, wishing I could somehow vanish.

With flushed skin, looking like she was mentally running through everything they had said that I might have heard, mom said, in a quavering voice, "go outside and play, Lito…" Sensing my uncertainty, she tried to reassure me. "It's okay, mijo. Go play." Dad didn't say anything.

I scurried through the living room, out the front door, to play, but I sensed then that something in my perfect world was wrong.

2

Summer came to an end on my first day of kindergarten. As mom and I were walking to my school, which was about ten-minutes from home, she schooled me on how to survive kindergarten. "Make a lot of friends today, okay?" she said.

Because I spent the first five years of my life with my family and nobody else, I didn't really know how to make friends. Biting my lip, I mumbled, "uh huh."

"And listen to your teachers, mijo," mom encouraged. "You're gonna have a lotta fun. You're the best boy ever."

Clutching mom's hand, I just listened as my insides quivered. "What if someone tries to hurt me?" The thought of not having my brothers or cousins with me unnerved me. I was going to be in a scary, unfamiliar place, with a bunch of strangers.

We made it to the entrance of the school, and mom kneeled down, smiling. She looked me in my eyes, and in a warm, caring tone, assured me, "you're gonna be okay, Lito." Tears welled up in my eyes as mom hugged me. My little heart was beating faster than the wings of a baby bird's first flight. "The day is gonna go fast, mijo. I promise." I clung to her. "And I'll be here to pick you up right after school. I promise. You're going to be okay."

Mom then stood up, pulled some tissue from her pocket, and wiped my face. "You ready?" Not really expecting a response, she grabbed my hand and led me into the classroom, toward the teacher.

Just before I could start crying, the teacher startled me with warm greeting, "Well, hello there!"

She knelt down, and gently put her hand on my shoulder. "Hi! I am so happy you are going to be in my class. What's your name?"

I hid my face in mom's stomach. I couldn't talk. Mom rubbed my head trying to calm me down. "Tell her your name, mijo. It's okay. This is your teacher."

I murmured, "Manuel Valentin Sarmiento." That teacher looked up at my mom for clarification, because there weren't very many people in Sterling with my complexion and that kind of name. Trying to help her out, mom said my name again.

I once asked mom how I got my name. She told me, "you are named after your dad, and you got your middle name from your great grandfather, Valentin."

My dad, Manuel, was born in a small village in Mexico. He immigrated to America, met and married mom. Mom said, "me and my sisters used to always say we were going to marry men from Mexico…to get closer to our roots, you know. So your aunt Molly got married to Beto's dad; aunt Gloria married Mara's dad; and, I married your dad. Before I met your dad, I used to always say I was going to name one of my sons Manuel. So when I met your dad, I thought it was meant to be."

When mom married dad, she made him "legal," giving him all the the rights and privileges of an American citizen. I remember him pulling out a laminated green card from his back pocket one day, and placing it in a drawer next to our living room couch. When he saw the curiosity in my eyes, he turned to me and said, "Mijo…Lito." I looked at him, sensing that he was about to tell me something important. He opened the drawer and pulled out the green card, and held it up, "You see this green card? You can never touch this, mijo. If you touch this, if you

lose this, daddy could go bye bye. The police are gonna
come and take daddy away, if you mess with this, mijo.
Comprendes (do you understand?)"

Not really understanding what he was saying, but
sensing the gravity of the situation- anything that would
make dad go away, in my young brain, was bad-, I just
nodded, "uh huh." I never did touch that green card,
although I opened the drawer from time to time, and stared
at it.

Mom determined that my middle name would be
Valentin. That was my great grandfather's first name.
Mom was the firstborn child of grandma, Blanca, who was
born in San Antonio, Texas to Valentin and Maria Guevara.
Grandma's story has always been a mystery to me, and to
anyone else I have asked. All I know is her father, Valentin,
was from Texas, and was the pastor of a small pentecostal
church in San Antonio. I don't know when he crossed the
border, or if he crossed the border legally. All I know is that
mom loved him, and enjoyed going to his church, partly
because the congregation was filled with people who
offered no shortage of entertainment for her and her sisters.
She always talked affectionately about my great
grandfather, and wanted to keep his name alive. So, when I
was born on June 23rd, 1977, at 6:07 A.M., I became
Manuel Valentin Sarmiento. That was the name I was born
with, and the name to which I answered for years.

Trying not to make a big deal out of my name, my
teacher just moved on, and said, "Man-well, we are going
to have lots of fun today. We're going to play games and
have story time and have snacks. Would you like that?"

I didn't have the nerve to tell her that she butchered
my name. Nodding, I said, "uh huh," then leaned into my
mom.

"Good, because I *love* games," she said enthusiastically as she escorted me to my seat while rubbing my back.

My nervousness slowly dissipated, and my breathing slowed down.

While sitting at my little desk, the bell rang, and the teacher introduced herself, standing in front of the class. "Good morning students...," she said. I don't remember her name, but I remember her pleasant demeanor.

With her hands clasped together, she walked closer to the first row of seats, with a warm smile and bright eyes. Her nurturing temperament put me more at ease.

"We are going to have a whole lot of fun, learn a lot, and make a lot of great memories together."

She walked toward her desk, "The first thing we are going to do is find out who is here today. When you hear your name, please raise your hand, and say 'here.'" She went through the list of names on her class-list, and the other kids promptly raised their hands, proudly announcing their presences.

Then, with her thick midwestern accent, she butchered my name. "Man-well Sarmiiiieaaaaaiiiiynto."

"Here," I said. Speaking in front of others felt like a big accomplishment for me.

After taking attendance, she laid laying down the law class rules, the bell rang. "It's recess," she said. "We are now gonna go outside and play. Who wants to go play?" The whole class rushed through the metal door, spilling out onto the playground. Many kids ran to the left, where the tether-ball and basketball courts were. I went to my right, where there was a tree-house with a slide and a jungle gym.

Once there, some of the other kids from my class decided to play a game of tag. Kids put one of their shoes into the circle, and the leader began, "Innie-minnie-miney-moe-catch-a-nigger-by-his-toe. If-he-hollars-let-him-go. Innie-minnie-miney-moe. My-momma-told-me-to-pick-the-best-one-and-you-are-not-it." Another boy was selected to be "it." Grinning, I popped up, and walked away swinging my arms in joyous delight.

As he counted to 10, we all scattered like roaches. The boy who was "it" tagged someone, and that person tagged another kid, and so on. Within the first ten minutes of playing tag, almost everyone but me had been tagged at least once.

"I'm way too fast for them," I said to myself, with a big grin on my face. The game went on like that for a while, and I still had not yet been tagged. In fact, no one even chased me. Wanting to get caught, adjusted my strategy, and began running half-heartedly, hoping to get caught, but none of the other kids ever came close to tagging me, because not one of them ever tried.

After about 10 minutes of being left out of the game, I drifted toward the monkey bars to play by myself. I grabbed the bar with both hands and began swinging back and forth, with my knees bent, and legs dangling.

A group of boys were running in my direction. I hung still in quiet expectation. "Maybe they're coming to ask me to play with them," I hoped.

The boys came to a halt about 3 feet in front of me, and the leader of the group, a white kid with blond hair, said, "Move out of the way, nigger!"

I lowered my feet to the ground, and stood up, staring at him, waiting for him to start laughing or something. He didn't. "Ha ha," confused, I laughed half-heartedly. I honestly had no idea what the word "nigger" meant. Yeah, it was a word that people in Sterling threw around, but, I guess because everyone around me often used the term in the context of games, it never occurred to me that "nigger" was a bad word. The white kid who was in my face, though, had used it differently.

He leaned forward, with a red face, and an intense, fevered stare, and flaring nostrils, and repeated himself, in a scathing tone, "*I said*...move out of the way, *you NIGGER!*"

I let go of the metal bars, mumbled something, then moved out of the way. I walked to the fence where mom dropped me off, and looked down the street as far as I could, hoping to see momma.

After recess, I returned to class, but I didn't really remember much more about the school day. The encounter on the playground just kept playing itself out in my head, over and over again. "What happened? Why were they mad at me? What did I do wrong? Why were they so mean to me? What is a nigger?"

After school, mom picked me up. "How was your first day of school?"

"Good."

"Were you a good listener?"

"Um huh," I nodded.

"You ready to go home?"

"Yeah." She took my hand, and we headed home.

While walking, I was kind of quiet. I mostly just nodded to whatever questions she asked.

We walked through the front door, into grandma's living room, but mom was concerned. "What's wrong, Lito? Are you okay?"

"Mommy, what's a nigger?" I asked.

She froze. Her mouth fell open, then she kneeled down in front of me, and looked me in the eyes...

3

"Did someone call you that, mijo? Did someone say that to you?" mom asked.

"Uh huh. A kid said to me, 'get out the way, nigger.'"

She turned red in her face. In her eyes, I saw rage and horror and sadness and fear and confusion. She looked at me, and said, "Baby, that's what mean people call black people."

I just stared at her.

She continued, "Who said that to you, mijo? You show him to me tomorrow. I'm gonna show them what a nigger is!" I didn't understand why she was so angry. I didn't know what she meant by black people. I just knew that momma was livid.

After she calmed down a bit, she sat down in front of me, and broke the news to me, "Mijo, your dad is black. Manuel is not your dad."

I just stood there looking at her. I had no mental categories into which I could place her words, but I felt something terribly wrong had just happened. "What do you mean, momma?"

She tried to make it more plain, "Mijo, your dad's name is not Manuel; your dad's name is Raymond."

Still, mom's words did not register in my brain. They made no sense whatsoever. "My dad is not my dad, but my dad is a guy named Raymond, who is black? What does all this mean?" My world was rocked.

I had my dad's name. His name was Manuel. My name was Manuel. I took pride in that. For five years, since my birth, he treated me like dad's treat their sons. He pinched my ears affectionately and called them "dulces" (sweets in Spanish).

Then, at five years old, the rug of my identity was yanked from under me, causing me to fall onto the back of my head, leaving me with a concussion of vertiginous questions: "Am I the reason mom and dad argue so much? What does it mean to be black? Is that why I'm more brown than everyone else in my family, and in Sterling? Is that why my hair is so curly, and nobody else's is? My mom is Mexican- in fact, everyone in my family is Mexican- but I'm black? How can I be something that my mom isn't, even though I came from her womb? Does that mean my ethnicity is determined by my father's ethnicity? By the way, who is my father, if it's not Manuel, the man I have been calling "dad" my whole life? Where is my father now, and where has he been all these years? Why have I never met him? Why has mom never told me about him until now? Does he even know I exist? Furthermore, is my identity and ethnicity something others assign to me (am I who others say I am?); or, is my identity and ethnicity something that I decide upon, and ultimately determine, myself (am I who I say I am, regardless of what others think about me)? Or, it is a little bit of both (am I who I say I am, as well as who others think I am)? Or, further still, is my identity and ethnicity something that exists independent of my, or anyone else's, opinion? A goat can believe that it's a cat all it wants, and others can tell the goat that it's a cat, but does that make the goat any more a cat? A goat is a goat regardless of what anyone thinks about it. Is that how my identity and ethnicity work? Also, why does it matter that I'm black, or latino, or white, or whatever? And, at the end of the day, who am I, and why does it matter?" While I was too young, at five years old, to ask, understand, or even answer those questions, mom's revelation that I was "black" gave birth to those kinds of questions.

For years, those questions lived with me, and stayed with me, wherever I went. When I moved, they packed their bags, and followed me. Like ghosts, they haunted me, and they refused to let me rest until I dared to address them with answers many years, and many tears, later.

So when mom broke that news to me, I couldn't speak. I didn't know what to say. So I just walked over to the couch and sat down. Life for me became as blurry as my identity.

One morning shortly after that conversation, mom woke me up by shaking me awake. "Mijo. Lito, wake up. It's time to get dressed." As soon as she saw me open my eyes, she stood up. "We gotta go," she said as she walked away. She was in a hurry. I sensed something was wrong, but I didn't know what.

I rolled off my floor mattress, and got dressed.

Mom had some brown paper grocery bags in her hands. She filled them with clothes and other things.

"Where are we goin', momma?" I asked.

"We are moving," she said. She walked out the front door, to a car. She put the bags in the trunk of the car, and then rushed back in to get more things.

"Momma, where are we going? What's wrong? Is dad coming with us?"

"Un uh. Let's go." What did she mean, un uh?

My heart dropped to my stomach. "But momma, I don't wanna leave dad." I pleaded while she kept walking back and forth past me to load more things into the car.

"I want dad to come with us. Momma I don't wanna leave dad."

After she loaded up the last bag, she glanced at her watch, then at me, "Get in the car, Lito. It's time to go."

"But momma, is Juan and Jose coming with us?"

"Not yet. They're gonna come later. Now get in the car," she said as she opened the back passenger door for me.

"But momma-"

"We gotta go, Lito! she interrupted. "Hurry up. Get in."

With my young mind and heart racing, I climbed into the car, and sat down.

"Hey Lito," aunt Molly said from the driver's seat.

I was too preoccupied with everything to respond. I just looked out the window to make sure mom was gonna get into the car too.

Mom got in. She sat down in the passenger seat, and closed the door. "Let's go Molly," mom said.

"Where are we goin momma?" I repeated.

"We're moving to Denver, mijo. We are going alone. Manuel is not coming. And stop calling him dad. He's *not* your dad."

My stomach tightened in disdain. "Yes he *is* my dad!" I protested, but didn't have the nerve to say that out loud. Many fond memories of me with my dad met me in the back seat of that car. Dad used to throw me up in the air and catch me. He used to hold both of my wrists and spin me in circles while I squealed with laughter. When he took our family to Mexico to visit his family, he gave me my first pet pig. He gave me piggy back rides. Dad taught me how to drink raw eggs so I could grow big muscles like him. Dad and I listened to Vicente Fernandez together. We watched Siempre en Domingo together. We laughed at

Cantinflas together. I wanted to be with my dad, and I didn't understand why mom was so set on separating us.

Aunt Molly started the car. I started crying. I turned around, and sat up on my knees, and stared at the house through the back window of the car, hoping dad would come out to stop us, or join us. But he could do neither because he wasn't home. So I watched helplessly, through a flood of tears, as the house got smaller and smaller in the distance.

Even the sun, like a brokenhearted child, refused to smile that day.

Sniffing, I wiped my runny nose with the collar of my t-shirt, and laid down in the back seat, squeezing my stuffed animal, Mr. Mouse, while the rivulets of sadness fell from my face.

4

A couple weeks after we moved to Denver, mom found a job and a place for us to stay.

"Hurry up, Lito. Get dressed. I'm gonna be late for work," mom said as she rushed back and fourth from her bedroom to the bathroom.

I put on my socks and pants, but my head got stuck in my tight sweater, that felt more like a straightjacket than winter apparel. "Momma, help! I can't breath!" I hollered.

Panicking, I bumped into the closet doors trying to free myself, "Mama! I can't breath. Help!"

She hurried over to me, "Your head's too big, man," she chuckled as she helped me push my arm through the sleeve, so I could get my head through the collar. Rubbing my head as she often did, mom said, "put on your shoes Mr. Wooly. I gotta go."

I was five, learning how to tie my shoes. "I can't do it, mama."

"Try harder. You can get it." Mom knelt down, tied my shoestrings into two perfectly symmetrical bows, then gave them one swift tap, letting me know she was done. "You gotta keep trying. You'll get it soon."

Then came her daily warning. "Don't talk to strangers. There are a lot of sickos out here. If anyone tries to talk to you, or tries to get close to you, Lito, run. Don't go to anyone's car, and if anyone tries to grab you, run. You fight if you have to, okay? Don't let anyone get you, mijo. You run fast."

"Uh huh," I nodded, opened the front door, walked outside, and as I headed down the stairs. I saw one of the hoops on my left shoestring was dangling. I didn't want to trip, so I knelt down, tucked it back into the hoop mama had made, and I hopped down the stairs. I walked to the corner, looked left, right, left, just like mama said, and I dashed across the busy intersection. Then I walked slowly for a block or so toward the old, small, tattered white house that I absolutely dreaded.

I abhorred going to that house because of what happened my first day, when mom dropped me off at her house. I knocked on the door, and after a few moments, it opened. "Buenos dias. Comm een," Maria said with her thick Spanish accent. Maria was a Mexican lady who agreed to babysit me while mom went to work. Mom didn't make enough money to put me in daycare, so she somehow got a favor from this lady. Maria spoke just enough English to say very basic things to me, but not enough to allay my fears of being left with a stranger.

"Comm," she said as she led me to her small living room, to an old, faded brown couch with sunken, bedraggled pillows that smelled like corn chips and vomit.

"Sientate." I just stared at her, fully aware that she was telling me to have a seat, but not really feeling comfortable about the whole situation. "Seeet down," she said, gesturing with her hands, pointing to the couch. Reluctantly, I had a seat. "T.V.?" she asked.

I nodded, "uh huh."

Right in front of the couch was a little brown, wooden coffee table with an upright picture frame, and in the picture was a soldier. In front of the coffee table was a very small black-and-white television with a copper hanger stuck into the barrel opening of where a metal antenna used to be.

"I'm een dee kee-shin," she said, as she walked toward the kitchen, and turned left, out of my sight.

Sitting on the edge of the couch, I stared at the picture on the little coffee table. It was of a young man, who looked about 18 years old, fully garbed in his green military attire, and posing in front of a poled American flag. He looked so proud, so strong, so young. Even though I was a little boy, I dreamed of one day becoming a soldier. I wanted to fight "the bad guys," and this young soldier's picture inspired me. I sat there, and began to imagine what his life was like as a soldier.

Moments later, I heard slow, dragging footsteps that sounded like sandpaper scratching along the floor. The footsteps were accompanied by moans. It sounded like a howling ghost was coming down the hallway toward the living room, toward me. I swallowed. "What is *that*?" I shrinkingly queried.

The hallway, where the noise was coming from, was between the living room, where I was sitting, and the kitchen, where Maria was cooking- there was *no way* I was going to cross that hallway, and risk getting anywhere near that dreadful sound!

Sitting on the edge of the couch, deathly still, I could feel my heart beating in my throat. I stared desperately toward the kitchen, hoping Maria would hear the sound, come out, and alleviate my fears.

The footsteps and the moans got louder, and drew closer. Then a man, in his mid-twenties slowly emerged from the hallway, hobbling with drool hanging from his mouth, like a great dane. His head was tilted so far to the right that his right ear almost touched his right shoulder. His right forearm, with drool all over it, and his twisted fingers, were awkwardly bent inwardly toward his chest. It was the same soldier from the coffee-table picture. But he no longer looked anything like his picture. As a little boy barely able to tie my shoes, I had no idea about the horrors of war, and what it does to real people. At that young age, I also lacked the compassion that such a veteran deserved. I was a kid, and I was horrified.

He twisted his eyes up toward me and made eye contact with me. I waved, hoping he'd be nice to me. But with a crooked, contorted smile, he flashed his brownish teeth at me, and moaned something. Terrified, I quickly looked away, hoping he would go away.

But he began hobbling toward me. I got up and ran to the corner of the room. He sped up. I felt trapped. I sprinted around him to an open door, into the bathroom. I slammed the door, and locked it with one of those little, metal door hooks. I then climbed into the bathtub and closed the shower curtain, and curled up into a ball, listening to the jiggling doorknob.

Moaning, he kept yanking the door, turning the doorknob back and forth, pushing, pulling, pounding, moaning.

I heard Maria in the background holler at him. The jiggling of the door stopped. And I just laid still in that tub trembling.

"Lito, eets ok. Lito, eets ok. He ees gone. He ees bye bye," Maria said through the door. I didn't move. I was frozen with fright. "Lito, eets ok. He ees bye bye. Abra la puerta…Open dee door."

I eventually came out of the tub, listened for that guy, and when I was convinced he was gone, I unlocked the door, and then backed away from the door.

Standing there, alone, Maria apologized, saying, "Sorry, Lito. He eees mi hijo…my son. Seeet down. See t.v." I wasn't interested in watching anything but that haunted hallway, so I just sat on that couch and kept eyeing it every few seconds. Every time I heard something, I jumped up, ready to run. Every time her son tried to come down the hall, Maria came out and scolded her son to go back to his room. I guessed he was trying to have a little fun with me, but I wasn't laughing.

After about thirty minutes, Maria walked over to me and asked, "tienes hambre?…Quieres comer?…You hoongry?." I nodded because I hadn't eaten breakfast. "Vente…come." She guided me over to her bare, round dining room table, and pointed at one of the three plastic chairs in which she wanted me to sit. I sat down and looked at a silver pot that was boiling on the stove. It had white, frothy foam spilling out from under its lid.

Maria walked to her cabinet, opened it, grabbed a bowl, and headed toward the stove. She pulled the lid off of the pot, and cockroaches began spilling over the rim of the pot, down its side, onto the stove! I got nauseous.

She saw the grimace on my face, and said, "Eeets okay. Eees okay, Lito. No worry." Her best attempt to assuage my concerns were not working. She picked up her metal spoon, scooped up some beans, and dropped them into a white glass bowl. She then poked around in the bowl with her fingers, and picked out several cockroaches. She dropped them into the trash can, then opened her silverware drawer, grabbed a small spoon, and brought the bowl to me. She placed it on the table in front of me. "Eeet, Lito. Esta bien. Eees okay."

I sat there absolutely appalled, with my stomach turning. I shook my head, and said, "no thank you. I'm not hungry. No thank you." "Eees okay, Lito. Eat."

I looked over to my left, and saw that her son had made his way back the living room. He was staring at me with that creepy, slobbery grin, and that devious look in his eyes. I can tell he was just waiting for the chance to play with me again.

I sat there at Maria's kitchen table, not budging, in front of my untouched bowl of beans and roaches. Neither hunger nor sleep were of any interest to me, because I needed to be ready to run, just like momma had told me. So I ran, every day, almost all day at that woman's home, until mom got off work, and rescued me.

5

It was around the fourth week of December, and only a couple months since we had moved from Sterling to Denver, when mom popped her head into the entrance of my bedroom. "Your grandpa's having a Christmas party," she said smiling, with her wide, pretty brown eyes.

Her words sped up a little as she asked, "You wanna go? You might get some presents, and your brothers are gonna be there too." Did I want to go? Are you kidding me? I started doing my crazy-legs dance. No music, no coordination; just very fast foot action. "Go Lito! Go Lito!" mom egged me on in laughter. "Oh my goodness, your legs are moving so fast!"

Then I tripped over my own legs, fell down, and trying to act like I did it on purpose, I rested my head in the palm of my hand. With a wide grin, I looked up at mom, whose eyes were gleaming, and I said, "Oh yeah!"

We didn't get to see grandpa that much because we lived in Sterling, and he lived in a suburb of Denver. But I guess with mom and me now living closer to him, and, since aunt Molly and aunt Gloria both lived in Denver too, he wanted us all to celebrate the holiday season together.

Grandpa, my mom's father, Mallory Lee Scales, was white, of Scotch-Irish and English descent. He was the great, great, great grandson of Joseph Scales Sr, a wealthy planter who owned 1800 acres and slaves. Many of Joseph's descendants fought in the military, from the Revolution to the Civil War. My grandfather, following that tradition, joined the military. He grew up in Galveston, Texas and enlisted as a teenager. In the Marines he was a Colonel. After his time in the Marines ended, he returned to

Galveston, and joined the Air Force, where he made it to the rank of Airman First Class.

In 1954, grandpa had become a Mess Attendant, serving meals and washing dishes at a military base in, or around, Galveston, where he met and married my grandmother, Blanca Guevara. They went on to give birth to my mom, Rose, my aunts Gloria, Molly, and Cynthia, and my uncle Johnny.

After being married for a little more than a decade, long before I was even a thought, grandma and grandpa divorced. Grandma moved to Sterling, and Grandpa stayed in Denver.

So at five years old, I didn't know, and didn't care to know, why or how grandma and grandpa separated. All I knew was grandpa had a new wife named Beverly, and, most importantly, that he was having a Christmas party where I would get some presents.

The day of the party, someone, I think aunt Molly, picked us up and gave us a ride to grandpa's party. My cousin Pedro, affectionately known to family as "Beto," was already in the car with aunt Molly. Everyone eagerly squeezed into aunt Nancy's car, and mom rode shotgun.

"Grandpa better hook us up," Juan said.

"You know, he's rich now that he's married to that rich white lady," Jose added. We all laughed.

"Yeah, but she's stingy," said Beto.

"I hope he gives me a $100," I added.

We had never been to grandpa's house, but word among the family was that he married up. On our drive to grandpa's, you could feel the excitement in the car.

Driving through all the immaculate neighborhoods, mom said, "man, guys look at all these nice houses."

"I know," aunt Molly said, "look at the front yards. The grass on all these houses is so green. There's no trash anywhere."

Jose said with excitement, "Grandpa is rolling in dough!"

"Man, all I know is, he better hook us up!" Juan exclaimed.

We pulled into the driveway, and we saw aunt Grace's car was already there. Mom and aunt Molly got out of the car, and pulled their seats forward so me, my brothers, and Beto could get out.

Everyone rushed to the front door, but nobody wanted to ring the bell first, because after all that talk about Beverly, we were all a little intimidated by her. "Who's gonna ring the doorbell?" Juan asked.

"Not me," Beto replied. "Lito, you ring it," he dared.

"No way! You do it," I deflected. Aunt Molly rang the stupid bell.

Mom was standing behind everyone else, to the right of the door, as if she was trying to hide. With her hand on my shoulder, mom asked me, "are you excited, mijo?"

"Uh huh, mama," I said, with bright eyes and hunched shoulders and a huge grin. "I can't wait."

After a few moments, Beverly opened the door. "Well, hello everybody!"

Everyone responded in unison, "hi!"

"Please come in," she said, gesturing for everyone to go into the living room where grandpa was sitting.

All my cousins and brothers rushed to grandpa, and hugged him. "What's up gramps?" Jose asked, as both he and Juan fell into grandpa's arms.

"Oh, nothing much boys," grandpa replied as he hugged them both at the same time. He was smiling from ear to ear as he hugged everyone. I never really spent much time with grandpa, so it wasn't natural for me to run and hug him.

Mom nudged me, "Go give your grandpa a hug."

I walked over to him, "Hi, grandpa." I gave him a hug, and he patted me on my back. The scent of his Old Spice aftershave followed me as I turned to play with my cousins and brothers.

"Now that everyone's here. Let's open some presents," grandpa said. Everyone gathered in the living room, and he began handing out wrapped gifts by name.

"Juan and Jose," he said as he picked up a box. After my brothers approached him, he handed them each a big box. They give him a hug, and thanked him. Grandpa then called my cousins Martha, then Jose, then Mara, then Miguel, then Bruno. They all hugged and thanked him. Everyone feverishly tore off the wrapping paper from their presents. Everyone was elated, ooing and awwing.

I looked over at the tree to see if there were any more gifts, but I didn't see any. I looked near grandpa's chair for a present, and there was nothing but torn wrapping paper. I looked at grandpa's face, and he was looking proudly at my brothers and cousins as they were all enjoying their gifts.

After a few minutes of everyone losing themselves in their gifts, I realized that grandpa didn't forget my gift; he left me out on purpose. Holding back tears, I quietly snuck out the front door, and I went to aunt Grace's car that was parked in the driveway. It was locked, so I sat down with my back against the passenger side door, so heartbroken that grandpa intentionally excluded me from his Christmas list. I felt so alone and unloved. I was devastated. What made things worse was that no one stood up for me. No one asked grandpa why he didn't get me a gift. No one. I cried outside for a while, but no one came out to check on me.

I sat there, alone. "Did no one else see what he did? Does no one care? Why did grandpa leave me out? What did I do wrong?" The questions persisted.

At 5 years old, I sat against that car door, crushed.

Shortly after that incident, I guess grandpa and Beverly had been having some marital problems, and grandpa needed a place to stay. So he came to live with me and mom. I was genuinely excited that I would have grandpa all to myself. Being a kid, I did not hold the Christmas thing against him.

One night, mom went out with some friends, and left me with grandpa to watch me. Grandpa and I were gonna have "guys night." I would get to be with him, and maybe he would tell me some of his war stories, or teach me something cool.

"You want some cereal?" grandpa asked.

"Yes, please," I said with excitement, because cereal for dinner meant we were about to have a good time.

Grandpa pulled out a white bowl and poured some generic frosted flakes into the bowl, and then poured the milk. He put the half-full gallon of milk back into the fridge, and then pulled out another bowl. He poured the cereal into it, then walked to the kitchen sink, where he turned on the cold water. He put water into my bowl and placed it in front of me at the table. He said, "We don't have enough milk for you." I took a bite, and put my spoon down, and just stared at him, confused. That cereal was terrible.

After he was done with his bowl of milked cereal, he asked, "you wanna play a game with me?"

"Um huh," I answered.

"We're going to play bull-fighting. You be the bull, I'll be the bull-fighter." He walked to the bathroom and grabbed a bath towel, then returned to the living room.

"You run as fast as you can to poke the towel with your horns, ok?"

I backed up, lowered my head, dug my hooves into the carpet, blew air through my nose, smiling, and sped toward the towel. He pulled it away just before I got to it, and hollered, "Ole!" just like a bullfighter.

I turned around, and he taunted me. I again dug my hooves into the carpet, smiling in my heart, and ran full speed at him. Again, as I was about to hit the towel with my lowered head, he pulled it away and laughed.

We did it a few more times, when he said, "c'mon you black bull! You can't get me!" I mustered up all my 5 year old playful rage, snarled at him, dug my hooves, and charged toward him at full speed. He didn't move the towel.

Bamm! I slammed head first into something hard and fell to the ground. "Owww!" Grandpa had positioned the towel in front of our hard, brass door knob. I looked up at his face, looking for comfort or assurance that I was okay, or for an apology, or concern, or something. With a smug look on his face, he stood up laughing and walked away.

My head was throbbing like I had been whacked with a baseball bat, and I felt a knot the size of a ping-pong ball forming on my head.

I was sitting on the floor next to the door, rocking and holding my head in pain, crying. Grandpa sat down on the couch and turned on the T.V, never once asking me if I was okay.

He acted like I was invisible.

Even though I was only five years old, I knew that grandpa meant to hurt me, but I didn't understand what I had done wrong. I didn't understand why, when I would walk past him, he would sometimes stare at me with hate in his eyes- the same look that was on the faces of those boys who called me a nigger on my first day of school. I didn't understand until later that my grandfather was infected with the malady of racism. That sickness caused him to often referred to my mom as "aunt Jemima" and "nigger-lover." That sickness also prompted him to try joining the Klu Klux Klan, but they denied his membership because, at the time, he was married to my grandma, who, according to them, was a "spick," a racist epithet coined for people of Mexican-descent.

6

We moved from place to place in Denver, landing in a basement apartment at 1084 Clarkson Street, now named the Camelot Apartments. I was about five, going on six.

In the apartment, I was doing my homework on a little brown coffee table in our living room. I was sitting up on my knees, struggling to write a lower case "a" . I asked mom for help, but preoccupied, she refused. While I was sulking, the phone rang.

Mom answered it. "Hello...oh hi!" Mom sounded surprised.

She walked to the kitchen with her back to me, and continued the conversation. The tone of her voice peeked my curiosity, and I began eavesdropping. She had a little smile on her face.

She continued, "Yeah, sure. When? Ok, I'll see you then."

She hung up the phone, and looked at me as though she was about to give me a surprise.

"Your dad is coming over."

"Dad?" I smiled, "he's coming from Sterling?"

"No. Your real dad, Raymond." I had mixed feelings. On the one hand, I was excited to meet my real dad. On the other hand, I didn't really know what was so exciting about that.

"He's coming over tonight so he can meet you...He knows karate, so he might show you some cool moves. Would you like that?"

That sounded exciting. I would be able to show off some of my skills, "Yeah, I'm gonna show him my side kick."

About an hour later, I heard three quick knocks on the door. My eyes widened with anticipation and I looked at mom. I jumped up and ran toward the door.

"Wait, Lito, let me make sure it's him." In our neighborhood, which wasn't the best, you needed to be sure who was at your door before you opened it.

"Who is it?" mom asked with a little bass in her voice to sound tough, just in case there was someone on the other side of the door with questionable intentions. After verifying his identity, my mom opened the door, and as the door swung open, I was waiting about 7 feet behind mom, but leaning forward to see this stranger who happened to be my father.

"Well, hello there," I heard him say. He was tall, six-two, to be exact, slender, had brown skin, and had a very warm smile. He leaned in and hugged my mom.

"It's so good to see you," mom said. She then looked toward me, directing my fathers attention to me as though she was saying, "there he is."

My father rushed toward me, reached down, picked me up, and squeezed me. "Oh wow! Hi son! Oh my God! You're so beautiful! He's so beautiful, Rose!"

While still holding me in his arms, he held me out in front of him, with my legs dangling, and he took a good look at me. Then he pulled me close to his torso again, and squeezed. He was so happy to see me, and I was somehow awkwardly happy that he was so glad to see me.

I was just staring at him, smiling. It felt good to be hugged like that. Something felt very natural and familiar about his hug.

He then put me down.

"Hi," I said as my eyes sparkled. "You wanna see my karate kick?"

"Of course!" he replied.

In the entrance area of our front door, I ran toward the door, leapt up as high off the ground as I could, and I put both of my feet up, flew toward, and struck, the door with both feet. I fell to the ground, and tried to break my fall with my arms.

"Wow!" he affirmed, laughing heartily.

I popped up unfazed. "You want me to do it again?"

Not wanting me to hurt myself, he asked, changing the subject, "you wanna see something cool?"

Mom, seeing that we were getting acquainted, walked to the kitchen to check on the food.

My father, barely twenty-two years old when I was five, did not really know how to relate to kids, so the first thing he taught me would probably never be included on a list of "Top Ten Things You Need to Teach Your Son." He knelt down, bent his forearm so that it touched his bicep, and he used his pointer finger and thumb to pinch in the crevice between his forearm and bicep into the shape of a woman's labia majora. He was using his fingers and arm to simulate the exterior of a woman's anatomy. Not knowing what it was, I just laughed, well, because my father was showing me something. Really, he could have showed me anything and I would have loved it.

He then moved on to something a little more age-appropriate. He pulled out a quarter, and laid it flat in his palm. He rubbed his hands together for a few seconds, and when he lifted his top hand, the quarter was gone!

"Whoa! Where'd it go?" I looked at mom astonished.

I was getting comfortable. "You wanna feel my muscles?" I queried. He touched my guns, and he acted blown away by how strong I was.

"Let me see how hard you can punch," he challenged, as he got down on his hands and knees, signaling me to punch his back. I wound up my arm and punched him as hard as I could, right in the middle of his left rib cage. He didn't like that game so much. I guess I whacked him too hard, because he became a little upset, insisting that I intended to hurt him.

Things went on like that between us for about thirty minutes. "I have to get ready to go to work, son, but I'll see you soon, okay?"

"Okay," I nodded.

When he stood up, and mom did too. He then picked me up and gave me another big hug, and said, "It is so good to see you, son. You are amazing." My young soul could feel that he meant it. I was so glad to meet him too.

He put me down and left.

It felt so good to meet my father. Although he had been absent for the first five years of my life, I felt an immediate bond with him. I could tell that he loved me. He had a kindness about him, a warmth, a love. When he looked at me, I felt his heart. I felt accepted. I felt like I belonged. When he picked me up, it felt right.

I was so excited to see what the future held for me and my dad.

A few days later, my mom and I walked into a huge auditorium that was abuzz with laughter. There was cigarette smoke and people around us were drinking alcohol. I had never been in a place like that before, but it seemed like a place that was for grown-ups only. There were anywhere between four or five thousand people in the building.

"Stay close to me, Lito. I don't want to lose you," mom said, holding my hand, guiding me through the crowd. We took our seats and the lights dimmed.

Then an announcer's voice over a loudspeaker said, "Coming to the stage is a rising star who has opened for Gary Shandling, Rosanne Barr, and…" The list went on… "Denver, make some noise for Raaaaaayyymmoooooonnnnnddd Grraaaaateee!"

"Raymond Grate?" I sat up, and looked at mom.

"That's him, Lito. Let's clap for him."

The crowd applauded, the curtains opened, and my father appeared. My father walked to the center of the stage.

"Thank you! It's so good to see all of you tonight."

He was opening for the legendary band, Earth, Wind, and Fire.

A bright spotlight followed him. With each joke, the laughter grew louder and louder.

"I love watching people fight," my father said as he set up his joke. "Have you ever seen someone who thinks he can fight, then get beat up? After they get hit in the face a few good times, they lose all composure." The crowd was with him. My father then acted out the joke, impersonating what a guy losing a fight looks like when he becomes desperate. My father closed his eyes and started swinging his arms all over the place. The crowd roared with laughter. Some people were cry laughing.

My father was the man! He knew how to grab the attention of an audience, and hold them in the palm of his hand. I saw several members of the audience doubled over in laughter because of things my father was saying. He seemed like he was having a great time, and the crowd was too. I sat there staring at him with so much pride and joy, thinking, "Wow! That's *my* dad!"

At the end of his set, my father walked off stage to a standing ovation. I sat there in awe. After the show, he came out to greet me and mom. He kneeled down and gave me a hug and a kissed me on the head. "What'd you think?"

"That was so cool! I saw you on stage in front of all those people! I was laughing at your fighting guy. That was funny!" I said.

He impersonated the guy for me again, just for me, an audience of one, and I laughed even harder than the first time he told the joke.

After that event, I hung out with my father a few times at his small, one-bedroom apartment where I watched him work on his comedic material. He didn't have a lot of furniture. Just a brown couch and a bed in the bedroom. Whenever I hung out with him at his place, I spent most of my time sitting on his couch, staring at him rehearse his set. He would say a joke over and over again, tweaking it, practicing it with different voice inflections, and tones, and body language; and, each little thing he changed about his delivery gave the joke a different feel. It was so fascinating to see him play with words.

He also had a thing for the arts. He picked me up from home one day, and took me to a photo shoot. We walked a few blocks and entered a warehouse that was being used as a photography studio. He introduced me to some woman who directed us to a dressing room. He helped me get dressed, but I was a little uncomfortable, because I had never really undressed in front of anyone. Things felt a little awkward. I managed to get the pants on, the shirt, and the suit jacket, and he helped me tie the tie.

The suit clearly belonged to a grown man several times my size, with a generous waistline.

"You look good, son," he affirmed, as he walked me across the warehouse floor, to a stack of crates arranged like stairs. Sitting at the top of the crates was a little girl who was wearing a grown woman's dress that was several sizes too big for her too. She was a pretty girl who looked Native American.

We sat there, and the photographer posed us, and snapped away, coaching us, "Put your arm over her shoulder. Nice." "Try to relax." "Smile…"

Once the picture was developed, my father gave me a copy to take home with me.

I also felt really proud to be wearing that suit. It felt like I was, in my father's presence, becoming a man. Him being in my life was not only transforming my outer appearance but my inner, self-perception. Subconsciously, the more time I spent with him, the more I believed I would be able to fill out that suit. With my father's help, I would one day become a man, and I would be big and strong just like him.

My father was a fighter. He had to fight his whole life, and he felt he needed to instill in me those same beliefs and skills, so that I too could survive. So he taught me how to fight. He walked me to the capital in Denver, and in the large grassy knoll there, my father showed me the basics of self-defense, "In life, son, you have to fight. People may try to hurt you, but you have to be able to take care of yourself."

My father showed me how to ball my fist up, and throw a solid punch, with my thumbs tightly folded under my index and middle fingers. "You always and only ever punch with your first two knuckles, straight ahead, or you could break your hand."

He even showed me how to do front kicks, side kicks, and roundhouse kicks. "Never kick anyone with your toes, son. You could break them, making it harder for you to fight. Try to strike them with the balls of your feet, or your heals. There's more power there, and you can do more damage."

I soaked it all in. It felt great spending time with my father, and learning from him.

"Son, you need to know how to block too." He then showed me inward blocks, outward blocks, upward blocks, downward blocks.

"And son, if someone is bigger than you, the best weapon you have is your feet. You run as fast as you can to a safe place...But if they catch you, and they have you cornered, then you hit them as hard as you can. In the nuts, in the neck, in the eyes, or in the nose."

Then he concluded our lesson with one final instruction. Son, you can also use your palm to break someone's nose, and push their bone up into their skulls. If you hit them hard enough, that'll get 'em off you son."

My father taught me, during our times together, things that have stayed with me my entire life. The most important thing he began to instill in me was a little bit of self-confidence, and the belief that I could survive any situation, if I had heart and determination. That belief would be tested just a few days later.

7

"How do I look?" mom asked, with her bright, dancing brown eyes and her beautiful, red, curled hair. As long as I can remember, mom had always had pretty, rusted red hair. She always had the longest, prettiest hair. In her teens, her hair was jet black, and went down to her lower back like the singer Crystal Gayle's, only not nearly as long. People often told her she resembled Cher and Barbara Streisand, and mom seemed to take pride in those comparisons.

"You look really pretty momma," I told her.

Mom lived for the weekends, because on Friday and Saturday nights, she would dress up nice and pretty, and go out to night clubs with her friends.

Before she left, she always gave me the talk. "I'm only going out for a little while. You can watch cartoons, but be really quiet so no one knows you're here. If anyone knocks on the door, hide. Don't open it. Do like I showed you. Go to your hiding place. If anyone finds you here by yourself, the police will take you away from me. So be careful, okay?"

While momma talked, worse-case scenarios crossed my mind: "Where would the police take me?" "Who would I live with?" "Would I ever get to see momma again?"

I swallowed. "Uh huh."

She turned on the T.V. "There might be some cartoons on right now. Try to find some."

Then she walked over to me, kneeled down, hugged and kissed me on the forehead. "I'll see you pretty soon."

"Okay momma," I responded.

"Don't stay up too late," she concluded. Then she walked out, and locked both locks from the outside.

I sat on the couch in silence, and worried for the rest of the night that mom might never come home. What if something happened to her? Who would I live with? Who would I call? Where would I go?

Whenever I heard a sound in the hallway, I turned down the T.V. I eventually fell asleep on the couch with the T.V. on.

At two or three in the morning, I heard keys in the door, and like I always did, I ran and crawled like a mouse into the small, dark opening under mom's waterbed, and listened for mom's voice.

I heard a scream. "Nooooooo!!!" It was momma. She was crying.

I froze under the bed to hear if anyone else was with her.

"No!!!" she screamed again. Her scream was so terrifying that it raised the hair on my arms, and compelled me to come out of my hole.

"Momma? What's wrong?" I asked while running to her.

Mom's hair was all over the place and eyeliner was running down her face. "Momma, what's wrong? Momma, what happened?"

She rushed past me to the bathroom and slammed the door. I followed her.

"Momma, what happened?"

"I'm okay, Lito, go to sleep."

"Momma, why are you crying? Tell me what happened?"

Still crying, she said "Lito, go back to sleep!"

I heard her crying through the door of the bathroom, and I just stood there, waiting for her to open the door.

The sobbing vacillated between sadness and rage. "That bastard! Awwwww!!!" Someone had hurt my momma.

"Momma, what happened?"

"Go to sleep. I'm gonna be okay."

Eventually momma came out of the bathroom, walked to the kitchen, and called someone. I just sat on the couch staring at her. Her blouse was ripped. She had scratches on her neck, and her hands were shaking.

Someone answered her call. "That bastard raped me! He raped me! He held me down, and he raped me!" she cried.

I didn't know what "rape" meant, but I could tell it was wrong. I balled up my fists just like my father taught me, thumb over pointer and index fingers.

Mom hung up the phone and went to the bedroom and laid down in her bed.

I laid on the floor next to her bed, hugging Mr. Mouse, and listened to my dear mother weep throughout the night.

On the floor, I kept wondering, "Where is my dad?"

8

I didn't know where my father was. "Why wasn't he here to protect mom?" He hadn't come by to see me for several days.

The next day, I walked to his apartment, and knocked on his door. No one answered. I knocked again, but still no answer. I went down the steps and squeezed between the bushes next to the porch, and I pulled myself up so I could look into the living room. Through the parted curtains I saw that the room was empty. There was no couch. There was no dad.

I lowered myself from the window.

I sat down on his front porch for at least an hour, waiting for him to come home. He never showed up. I was confused because he never mentioned anything to me about him having to go anywhere.

When I finally got home, I told mom what I had seen. With a puzzled look on my face, I reported, "Momma, I went to my dad's house, but I couldn't find him."

Mom took a deep, pained breath. "Son, he's not going to be coming around any more. He had to go away."

"Why?" "Where'd he go?"

"Um, I don't know," she replied.

"But momma-"

"I know baby…I'm sorry."

Holding back tears, I walked into mom's bedroom, and collapsed onto my mattress on the floor, clung to Mr. Mouse and the picture my father gave me of me in the oversized suit. I buried my face in my pillow, and I cried inconsolably. I didn't understand. I thought to myself, "Why did he have to leave me?" "Why does everyone keep leaving me?" "Is something wrong with me?" Even though it probably wouldn't have made things any easier, I still wished that he would have at least told me why he had to leave; and, if nothing else, to tell me goodbye.

9

Not long after mom was violated, and after my father disappeared, we moved again, into the projects in downtown Denver, which were a couple blocks away from the old training camp of the Denver Broncos. The projects have since been torn down, but my memories of our time in them still stand in my mind.

Despite the challenges of living with limited financial resources, my mother always had a beautiful way making the most of life. She was also an excellent salesperson who could persuade you to buy whatever she was selling. Those things, joined to perhaps mom's greatest attribute, her hilarious, and sometimes twisted, sense of humor, gave me no shortage of funny moments.

For example, when I was seven years old, mom convinced me to let her dress me up as a girl for Halloween. "Baby, what do you want to be for halloween?"

"I want to be superman, or batman."

She got all bright-eyed and sat up straight. "What if we do something different; something that sets you apart from everybody else? It'll be cool."

"Okay. Like what?"

"Let's dress you up as a little girl."

I think my jaw fell to the floor, "What? Awww naawww, momma. I don't wanna be no girl for halloween." She couldn't be serious.

She laughed, then began making her case. "You know I've always wanted a little girl." She tilted her head to the side and flashed her puppy-dog eyes at me. "You can be my little girl. You're my baby. Just this once for me. We can dress you up really nicely, and make you look really pretty, and nobody would even be able to tell."

I couldn't believe it. "No way! I don't want to be no little girl, momma," I said as I glared at her. "That's not cool, momma. I wanna be something cool like Superman, or Batman." To be honest, at that point, I would have been willing to be a roach for halloween. But a girl? Heck no! I was only seven years old, but I had to draw the line somewhere.

"You know what else?" she asked.

I was shaking my head back and forth, because momma had pretty much lost all her credibility with me by then.

"Hear me out," she said.

I wanted to get out of that conversation as quickly as possible, but out of respect for mom, I glanced at her uneasily.

"People give more candy to cute little girls than they give to superman, mijo."

She got my attention, but I was still reluctant. "I don't wanna be no girl, momma."

"You want a lot of candy, don't you?"

I nodded uneasily.

"I'm telling you, dressing up like a little girl would get you more candy, and it'll be really fun, and nobody will know that it's you," she said, smiling.

"Nobody can know, momma," I capitulated.

We went to the little store on the corner and picked up our accessories.

Mom put a long, jet-black wig on me that went down my back, past my butt, and she put black eyeliner around my eyes, and bright red lipstick on my lips. Then, to bring it all together, I guess, she put a pair of her black, shiny, patent-leather pumps on me. I was wearing 3-inch heels. And they dragged when I walked.

"Wow! You look soooooo preettttyyyyy!" mom said as she tried to keep me from changing my mind. "You are gonna get a lot of candy tonight! You ready?"

Staring at her through my long black bangs, I searched her face for the slightest reason to not go forward with her plan. "I don't know about this, momma…"

"It'll be fun. Let's go before it gets too late, and people run out of candy," she said, smiling, a little too big.

She escorted me to one of the nicer neighborhoods in the area so we could get some of the good, "rich-people" candy. She walked me up to the first home's front lawn, and coached me on what to do when I got to the door.

"When you get up there-"

"Are you coming with me, momma? I want you to come with me."

"No, you gotta go by yourself. You can do it, Lito… They'll give you more candy if you go by yourself…So, when you get to the front door, ring the doorbell, and then wait for them to open it. When they open the door, say 'trick or treat,' and put your pillow case out so they can put candy into it for you." She was so persuasive.

I eased toward the door, as a girl in high-heels and bright red lipstick, trying to convince myself that it was worth it.

You could hear the heels scraping on the brick walkways with each step I took. I did everything mom told me to do. When the door opened, an older white woman greeted me, smiling from ear to ear.

Mom and I never talked about my voice. In that moment, I felt my testosterone ask, "are you gonna talk like a boy, and give yourself away, and give up your manhood;

or, are you gonna talk like a girl, and get more candy, and give up you manhood?" I was in a lose-lose situation.

I took a deep breath, and said in a breathy falsetto voice, "trick or treat." It felt so degrading. But I had to go through with it.

"You're just the prettiest little girl! Here you go sweetheart!" She dropped candy into my pillow case, and I just stared at her, waiting for her to express how impressed she was at my ability to conceal that I was a boy.

She said, "have a good night little lady," and closed the door.

That felt really uncomfortable. I took that long walk of shame down the walkway trying to figure out what I had gotten myself into.

"Good job!" mom said. "See, she didn't even know, did she?"

"No."

"See, and you got some candy in your bag too, right?"

"Um huh."

Despite mom's verbal reassurances, she had the biggest, I-really-want-to-bust-out-laughing-at-you smile on her face. "Let's go to the next house and do it again."

Trying to block out the chagrin, I went from house to house, filling my pillow case with candy. However, I started getting upset because no one could tell I was a boy. So, to salvage the tiny vestiges of manhood I had left, I started using my boy voice to say "trick-or-treat." Still, no one noticed I was a boy.

I had had enough.

One woman opened her door, and said, "You're so pretty."

I raised my voice and declared, "I'm a boy!"

She looked startled, and trying to contain her laughter, just said, "okay." She glanced up at my mom, flashed a quick smile, then dropped candy into my bag, and closed the door.

While I was walking away from her door, I could hear that woman laughing.

I was fuming.

To make an already pleasant night even more delightful, my mom took me to a halloween party at the projects' community center. Sure enough, all the other boys were dressed up as robots, and superman, and other macho things, and the girls were princesses and Tinkerbell and so on. And there I was, walking around with a big black wig on my head, wearing three-inch pumps. I was so self-conscious I sat out of all of the the festivities. And besides, the pumps were too hard to run in anyway.

10

As gifted as mom was to make a joke out of anything, there were some things about living in the projects that weren't so funny.

One night, mom and aunt Molly were driving around the projects trying to find someone from whom to buy some marijuana. I didn't know what "weed" was, but I didn't want to stay home alone while they went looking for it. So I just rode silently in the back seat, looking out the window at the people, and the street lights. In the projects, it always fascinated me how no one came out during the day, but they packed the streets at night.

"Turn here," mom said to aunt Molly. It was a dark street with only a few street lights. In the distance mom saw something.

"Is he hitting her?" mom asked.

Aunt Molly slowed down to get a closer look.

I sat up, and looked through the front window.

A husky man was yanking a woman around like a rag-doll, and slapping her. I think he was her pimp. I don't remember getting a clear look at him, but I could clearly see that the woman being beaten was white, and was scantily clad, wearing a mini skirt, high-heels, and a small jacket.

"I'll kill you!" I heard him yell.

Trying to pull away from him, she was crying, and pleading, but he had a tight hold on her jacket with his left hand, and with his right hand he slapped her so hard that I could hear the smack through our closed car windows.

"Pull over, Molly!" mom demanded. "Right next to them!"

"Are you sure, Rose?"

She pulled the car up so we were about 15 feet away from them.

Mom rolled down her window, "Hey! Leave her alone!"

I ducked down in the back seat.

The pimp looked at mom with rage in his eyes. "Mind your own business."

"Now let her go before we call the police."

The woman spoke up. "I'm okay. It's okay."

"No, you're not. That's not okay. You wanna come with us?"

The pimp had something to say about that. "You must be crazy. Get outta here, or I'll beat your behind too!"

"You and what army?" mom said as she reached under her seat, opened the door and got out of the car.

"Momma, get back in the car!" I begged.

Aunt Molly got out too. Mom walked toward the man with a short black metal bar in her right hand. Aunt Molly walked around the front of the car slightly behind the man's back.

Sensing that he was about to get attacked, the pimp let go of the woman. He then faced mom, and watched aunt Molly out of the corner of his eye.

"What you think you gonna do with that?" the pimp asked.

"Let her go. She's coming with us."

"Like hell she is."

Mom looked at the woman, "Come with us. It's okay. He shouldn't be hittin' you like this."

The woman took a step away from her pimp to see what he would do. He didn't move. Then she took another step closer toward the car. The woman jumped into the passenger side, slid to the middle of the front seat, and mom and aunt Molly jumped back in the car, and sped off.

"See you later, asshole!" mom hollered as we drove off.

The woman was crying. "Oh God! Thank ya'll so much. Thank ya'll so much!"

Her lip was bleeding.

"I'm Evelyn," she says. "God, thank ya'll so much."

"Yeah! We showed him. Girl power!" mom laughed.

"Rose, you're crazy," aunt said.

"What? I would have clobbered him if he tried anything."

They all laughed.

I sat in the back seat, relieved.

"Where should we take you?" mom asked.

"To my apartment."

"Are you sure? Does he know where you live?"

"I'll lock the doors."

We pulled up to her building, which looked very familiar- she lived in the same projects as us, about thirty yards from our front door.

Everyone got out the car. Evelyn thanked mom and Molly again, and she limped to her apartment, went inside and closed the door.

11

My brothers, Juan and Jose spent most of their time with grandma, but they would occasionally visit us while mom and I lived in the projects. One night we heard a woman's scream through our bedroom window, "Call the ambulance! PLEASE HELP!!!" Startled by the desperation of her voice, we peeked through the curtains, and saw a crowd gathering on the sidewalk and in the street.

Juan said to Jose and me, "Let's go see what's going on? It looks like someone is laying in the street." Though we had each other, Mom never let us go out after dark in that neighborhood. She often said it was too dangerous, but we took our chances every now and then.

Juan unlocked the doorknob, deadbolt, and the chain-lock on our back door, and walked outside. Jose stepped out after him, and I followed behind Jose.

We walked toward the crowd, and could see that people were very upset.

The closer we got to them, we noticed the crowd had formed a circle around someone in the street. It was a black male, in his early twenties. He was lying on his back. There was blood all over the street, and blood all over his face. It oozed out of his mouth. He was shaking, and gargling. He looked so desperate, and helpless. His eyes were wide open and he wasn't blinking. It was such a terrible sight.

"Somebody, please help him! Oh my God! Please help him!" a woman screamed. But there was nothing anyone could do to help the man. Neither doctors nor nurses, or police lived in our neighborhood.

People became restless, screaming, "where are the police? Where is the ambulance? He's gonna die!"

Jose found a familiar face in the crowd and asked him, "What happened?"

"A car hit him while he was crossing the street. He went face first into the windshield, and was thrown from the hood of the car onto the street. Then the car sped off. It looked like he meant to do it. It's messed up."

"Yeah, that's messed up," Jose replied.

I was standing by the man in the street, staring at him. Anger started welling up in my heart. "Where is the ambulance? It's taking too long! Why are they taking so long? If they don't come, he might die."

The man's eyes rolled back into his head, and he died.

It was in the projects, seeing things like that happen over and over again, that I began to understand why so many people had so little faith in those who were paid "to protect and serve" us. In our predominantly black and latino neighborhoods, when people called 911 for help, it was not uncommon for the cops or the ambulance to show up too late, and, sometimes they didn't even show up at all.

A few weeks later, I was snatched out of my slumber in the middle of the night by a bolt of lightning that sounded like it struck something right outside my bedroom window. I cleared my eyes and rushed to the window. It was raining so hard it looked like millions of fire hoses were spraying from the sky.

Then another bolt of lightning crashed down about thirty yards from my window. I collapsed back onto my bed, pulled my blanket over my head, plugged my ears, and closed my eyes.

I laid there in the fetal position until the storm calmed.

Then I heard another sound. Bam! Bam! Bam! "It's just the wind," I thought. Then again, the second time the bams became faster- Bam! Bam! Bam!... It wasn't the wind. Faster and harder. Bam! Bam! Bam! Bam! Bam! The sound was coming from downstairs, from our living room. It was about two or three o'clock in the morning.

I was scared. I heard mom's door squeak open. With the lights still off, I peeked out of my room. Mom's eyes darted to me. She whispered, "Quiet, Lito."

Bam! Bam! Bam! Bam! Someone was pounding on our front door.

Mom began tiptoeing down the stairs. I followed mom down the stairs, scared.

Bam! Bam! Bam! Bam! Bam! The pounding grew louder and more urgent.

We got to the bottom of the stairs, and mom stopped in front of the door. I walked passed mom, and stood behind her a couple feet to her left.

Bam! Bam! Bam!

"Who is it?" mom yelled, trying to sound tough.

Bam! Bam! Bam! Bam!

"Help me!" we barely heard someone say, because the rain was coming down hard again.

Mom tried again. "Who is it?"

"Please, open the door!" a woman's voice pleaded.

Mom rushed to kitchen, grabbed a knife from the drawer. I followed her, and grabbed one too.

Mom returned to the door.

Bam! Bam! Bam! Bam!

"Back up, Lito."

Mom removed the chain from its latch, then unlocked the deadbolt. She turned the doorknob. I held my breath.

It was one of the most terrifying sights I had ever seen. Standing on our doorstep was a bloody woman whose hair was pasted to her face like clumps of seaweed. Her eyes were swollen shut and her lips were busted wide open. Her face looked worse than any beaten boxer I have ever seen. We did not recognize her.

"Rose!" the woman mumbled, then stumbled forward into mom's arms. Mom caught her.

"Evelyn?!?! Oh my God!"

"Hurry, he's coming. Close the door, Rose! He's coming! He's coming!"

Evelyn looked at me. I stood there, in shock.

Mom looked at me. "Go to your room, Lito." She didn't want me to see any more.

I ran up the stairs to my room, but felt compelled to sneak back down so I could eavesdrop.

Evelyn was crying uncontrollably.

"He's coming, Rose. He knows I'm here. When he doesn't find me at home, he's going to come over here."

I squeezed my knife.

Mom got up and double-checked that she had locked the door.

When she did so, she saw me on the stairs.

"I said go to bed! It's okay." she intoned.

"But momma, she said-"

Mom cut me off, "It's okay. I'll come get you if I need your help."

I stood up, I went to my room, and left my door cracked open so I could listen. I got under my covers. While lying there, my mind wandered. I could not understand why anyone would do that to another person. I didn't need any ethicist or expert to tell me it was wrong. In my heart, I just felt someone had done something terribly wrong to that woman.

I laid in bed concerned, but mostly scared. "What if whoever did that to her comes to our house? I fell asleep with that knife under my pillow.

Mom and Evelyn became good friends, and a month or so later, mom took me to a house party at Evelyn's apartment. We walked in, and smoke was everywhere. Weed and cigarette smoke filled the room. People were staggering around with drinks in their hands. Some people were sitting together on the couch and engaged in conversations. Others were standing around, in corners, in the kitchen, and on the stairs. Everyone was talking, smoking, drinking, and laughing. Some were even making out.

"Lito, why don't you go upstairs, and see if Evelyn's daughter is here," mom said.

Evelyn's daughter was sitting on her bed. She was about a year older than I was.

"Hi. My mom told me to come up here."

"Come in. What's your name?"

"Manuel."

"You wanna watch T.V. with me?"

"Uh huh."

After watching a little television, she wanted to play another game.

"You ever played house?"

"Nu uh, what's that?"

"Get under the bed, and I'll show you."

Sounded like fun to me.

She crawled under the bed with me. "You're the daddy and I'm the mommy. You do what daddy's do and I'll do what mommy's do."

I had no idea what dad's did, so I just laid there. But she began rubbing on my chest, and hugging me. I went with the flow and hugged her back. Then she started simulating a french kiss with me, sticking her tongue out and closing her eyes. I did the same thing, not knowing what I was doing.

We heard someone coming up the stairs, but did not have time to come out from under the bed fast enough, so we stayed still when her bedroom door opened. Then it closed. I guess someone was checking on us.

I waited a few seconds, then I came out from under the bed.

After hanging out in that room for a while, I went to look for momma. I walked through the house looking for momma, but I couldn't find her. I figured she had gone home, looking for me. So I started heading through the kitchen, toward the front door. Evelyn stepped right in front of me. She was holding a cigarette in one hand, and a beer the other.

"What are you doing?" she asked.

"Lookin' for my momma."

"Your momma's not here," she said in a sarcastic, condescending tone.

My eyes scanned the room, looking for mom.

I then tried to step around Evelyn, but she moved in front of me again, blocking me from leaving. I looked up at her, confused. She then raised her right arm, and smashed her lit cigarette onto my face, burning me a few millimeters above my left eye. I yelped, put my hand over my eye, and began crying.

Evelyn laughed and walked away.

I ran home, looking for mom. She wasn't there. Crying and in pain, I ran to the fridge, opened the freezer, and grabbed a piece of ice for my burn. I walked upstairs looking for mom in her bedroom, but still couldn't find her. I then got into my bed, and laid there crying.

Tears of sadness. Tears of anger. Tears of loneliness.

But while I was on my bed, I felt something strange. I felt a warm presence come near me. I didn't understand it, but it did not scare me. The presence actually felt very safe, very loving, and extremely warm. With my head under my covers, there was someone, or something in the room with me that was comforting me. The presence didn't say anything, but in my heart I felt like it was saying, "You are not alone. I am with you." As strange as that may sound, I can say beyond of a shadow of a doubt that something, or someone, very real visited me in my bedroom that night. It was outside of my mind. It was not a hallucination. Something beyond me, outside of me, entered my room that night. That indescribably comforting presence comforted me in ways I cannot describe. Eventually, in the presence of whatever, or whoever that was, I fell asleep.

12

Shortly after that incident, Mom grew tired of the projects, and moved us into a lime green trailer in Aurora, a suburb of Denver. The trailer park is gone now, but it is not too far from the Fitzimmons Army Medical Center in Aurora. We moved next door to grandma, who had moved from Sterling to Aurora to be closer to her children and grandchildren. Aunt Gloria also lived in that same trailer park, a few rows over. After feeling isolated in the projects, I was relieved to be closer to my family again, with Miguel, Mara, Martha, and my brothers.

Mom enrolled me at Vaughn Elementary School in Aurora, where I started third grade. That first day of school I walked with a little pep in my step, because I believed that I would enjoy attending Vaughn because my cousins, Mara and Miguel, would be there too. Although we were in different grades, it just felt good to know I would be in the same buildings as my family.

Mom walked me into class, where Mrs. Elliott, a wonderful, red-headed teacher warmly welcomed me. I think her red hair comforted me because it resembled both grandma's and mom's hair.

Before class began, I sat down at my desk, and looked around at all of the pictures on the wall. The bell rang, and Mrs. Elliott, with her black-rimmed, rectangular glasses and bright smile with pearly white teeth, greeted us.

"Well, welcome kiddos! I am so happy to meet you, and I am so grateful each and every one of you is in my class this year." Her enthusiasm and charisma rubbed

off on us. I too was glad to be in her class. She seemed
really kind and loving.

"Since it is the first day of school, we are going to
play a game. Who likes games?" Wide grins came across
our faces, and my eyes gleamed, and we all threw our
hands in the air, "I do! I do!"

"Good! Here's the game. You are going to tell
everyone your first name and last name, and then you are
going to tell the class about the most fun thing you did this
summer. I'll go first."

She set the tone for the class so well, "My name is
Mrs. Elliott, and I just love the Denver Broncos," she said
as she began walking over to a brown, oak cabinet. She
opened it, and pulled out a big, brown football. "I went to a
Broncos game this summer, and I sat right behind the field
goal post in the end zone; and the kicker, Rich Karlis,
kicked a field goal, and the ball came straight to me, and I
caught it!" We, the students, all knew who Rich Karlis was,
because all of us were Bronco fans, and our kicker, Karlis,
always kicked the football bear-footed, even in the middle
of games played in winter.

My eyes widened, and I sat there staring at the ball.
"No way! You caught a ball that Rich Karlis kicked?!
Wow!" We all leaned in, hoping to get a closer look at the
ball.

"I'll pass it around if you all promise to take really
good care of it."

"We won't drop it. Promise!" many kids assured.

"Okay, here it is," she said as she handed it to the
student in the front row of the class. When it got to me, I
couldn't believe that I was actually touching a real NFL
football. I was so inspired, because I wanted to play for the
Broncos when I grew up. That was my dream.

After we all admired the ball, she retrieved it, and said, "That was the best part of my summer." She then placed it back into her cabinet, closed the door, and locked it with a key. Mrs. Elliott turned around and asked, "Who wants to go next?"

Other kids' hands shot into the air. She called on one of them, a boy. He said, with a proud look on his face, "My family and I, we went camping, and swam in the lake, and had campfires, and burned marsh-mellows...That was the best part of my summer."

That sounded like a lot of fun. "What can I share about my summer?" I thought to myself. Others continued.

"Very good," Mrs. Elliott affirmed. "Who's next?" She called on the next kid. He sat up straight and said, "I went fishing with my daddy and my granddaddy. We saw deer and elk. It was so much fun!"

I awkwardly mirrored the behavior of others.

"Very good. Next?" She looked at me, but I quickly looked away. Thank goodness she called on someone else.

"Me and my family went to Disneyland in California. We caught the airplane, and saw Mickey Mouse and Minnie Mouse and Pluto and rode all the rides. It was my best summer ever!"

"Wow! Sounds like you had a lot of fun. Very good. Thank you for sharing. Next?" I looked down, really thinking hard about something fun I could share with the class.

Another kid didn't wait for Mrs. Elliott to call on him. He boasted, "My parents bought me a Nintendo video game system for my birthday, and bought me a bunch of video games like wrestling, basketball, and football, and Mario Brothers. I played the games all summer, and even beat the game."

"Next?" Mrs. Elliott asked. A little girl shared her experience. "My mommy and daddy took me to London, and we rode the big ferris wheel, and we saw the Parliament building, and we saw the big giant clock called 'Big Ben.' And we went sightseeing all over the United Kingdom. We take trips like that every summer."

Mrs. Elliott chimed in. "Wow! You guys had a very nice summer. Does anybody else want to share the highlights from your summer?"

I looked around at the other kids, and felt like they were living in a different world than I was. I hadn't done anything close to the kinds of fun things they had done over the summer- I saw someone die. I saw a woman almost get beaten to death. I had a cigarette put out on my face.

So I sat there, self-conscious and quiet, hoping Mrs. Elliott wouldn't call on me. That self-consciousness took up residence in my mind the rest of my time in that class. It seemed like everyone else had more than I did. It felt like the other kids were better than I was; that I was not as good as them. And some of them even treated me like I was less than they were.

For example, one day Mrs. Elliott, told us to pull out our geography books from our desks, and she started a geography lesson about the continent of Africa.

"Open your books so we can read aloud. Let's start in the front left of the class." The first student read a paragraph, and then Mrs. Elliott picked volunteers to read the following paragraphs, one at a time. I never raised my hand to volunteer. I didn't want to sound stupid in front of everyone, because I couldn't read as well as they could. I could read slowly, but it took me a little more time to sound out the words. I always jumped ahead one paragraph to begin practicing the words that were unfamiliar to me, so that if I were called on by the teacher, I would be ready to read without embarrassing myself. On that day, I saw a word in the upcoming paragraph that made me very uncomfortable. "Niger." It was a reference to the Niger River in Africa, but I had never seen it before, so I thought it was pronounced "Nigger." The word re-opened an old wound for me, and I sat there nervously. I was the only kid in my class with brown skin, so I became even more self-conscious.

As the class got closer and closer to reading that word, Niger, I began to feel more and more uneasy. I wondered, "Why would they call that river that name? That's a bad name. That's the same name that that kid called me in Sterling." Sure enough, when the kid who was reading got to the word, he said, "The Nigger River is the third-longest river in Africa…" Some of the students chuckled. I shrunk in my seat.

Mrs. Elliot corrected him. "It's actually pronounced, 'Ny-jur River.'" I felt a little relief, and I peeked up at her, and saw Mrs. Elliott glance over at me to see if I was okay. While her sensitivity toward me seemed very real and genuine, there were some things from which Mrs. Elliott could not protect me.

I guess with all my moving about, I had been falling behind in school, and about two months into the semester, my deficiencies had become painfully clear. I was sitting in Mrs. Elliott's class, and she opened the class with a question.

"I need some people to volunteer to tell me what helping verbs are."

Almost twenty hands shot up, which was great for me, because that meant I could hide in the crowd. One kid quickly said something like, "Helping verbs help main verbs, and they come before the main verb. Helping verbs help verbs get more done."

"Very good. Now can someone tell me what the helping verbs are?"

She called on a kid in the front row, who responded, "Am, is, are, was, were; be, being, been; has, have, had; do, does, did; will, shall, should; would, can, could; may, might must."

"Well that was easy! Congratulations!" she said as she handed the kid a sticker.

"Next?" She called on each student, one by one, while I sat there, in the back of the class, silently hoping that someone else- at least one other kid- would get them wrong. To my chagrin, each and every one of my classmates before me let their helping verbs flow out of their mouths like water. I had never heard of helping verbs, and certainly had never seen a list of the helping verbs that everyone else was reciting. But I tried to memorize them as I heard each kid going through them. I mouthed, "Am, is, are, was, were..." then I got stuck.

The next kid would start, and I would try to follow, "am, is, are, was, were, has..." I just couldn't keep up. I couldn't retain the words fast enough. One student after the other, with poetic fluidity danced through the words: "Am, is, are, was, were; be, being, been; has, have, had; do, does, did; will, shall, should; would, can, could; may, might must."

With every successful recitation, my foot began to tap faster, and I began to sweat. Even the kids who were normally quiet in class were getting them right.

Mrs. Elliott was getting closer and closer to the back of the room, where I sat. "Please don't call on me.

Please don't call on me. Please don't call on me," I hoped in my heart.

She called on me, "Man-well, your turn. What are helping verbs, and recite them for me, honey."

My face, neck, and ears felt impossibly hot, and my heartbeat sped up. My mouth would not open, so I just stared at her, in fear.

"Man-well, can you recite your helping verbs for me, please? You can do it." She started them for me, "am, is, are, was, were- now you finish them for me."

I swallowed, my chest tightened, and I looked around for help, and strained to say something, but I just couldn't. I couldn't speak. I didn't know what to say.

"Do you know any of them?"

Tears welled up in my eyes, and sobs were trapped in my throat. I shook my head back and forth, and softly murmured, "uh uh."

Mrs. Elliott sighed, disappointment visited her countenance long enough for me to see it.

I put my head on my desk, with my face in my arms. I felt so worthless. "Why don't I know these like everyone else?" I pouted inwardly. "Is something wrong with me? Why don't I know what helping verbs are, but everyone else knows them? Is something wrong with me? I must be stupid or something!"

Those feelings of inadequacy were regular guests in my mind, and teased me whenever I thought about school. School for me began to feel like prison. I felt like it was a place where I was constantly reminded of how stupid I was, how far behind I was, how much worse I was than the other students. School for me began to mean pain and shame, so, like any sane person, I started thinking of ways to get out of going to school.

I often resorted to desperation. One snowy morning, I decided that I did not want to go to school.

So I hid my shoes in my closet, under the huge pile of dirty clothes that was at least four-feet tall. I went into mom's bedroom where she was still asleep, and said something that I hope will cause her to give me permission to miss school. "Mom, I can't find my shoes."

"Go look everywhere, Lito. They're here somewhere."

"Okay." I acted like I was looking for my shoes, trying to stall long enough for me to miss the first bell at school. I just knew that she would not make me go to school without my shoes.

After 15 minutes, I returned to mom's room. "Mom, I can't find them. I guess I just have to stay home, because I'm already late for class."

"No! You go find your shoes right now. Where did you last see them?"

"I don't know, momma."

"Well, go look, because you're going to school, Lito."

"But momma, I can't find them. I looked everywhere."

"You're not missing school, Lito. Go find your shoes, man!"

I got up and walked out of mom's room, and continued to feign my search.

She started looking too. Mom walked into my bedroom, and looked under my bed. Then she walked to the living room and looked under the couches. "Lito, if you can't find your shoes, then you are going to have to go to school without them."

"But momma, I looked everywhere. I can't find 'em."

"You better find your shoes, Lito, or you're walking to school without them."

"But it's snowing, momma."

"Then find your shoes!"

I sped up my pace, looking in the same places over and over again, but still coming up empty-handed. I glanced at the clock, and saw that school had already started. "Yes!" I thought to myself. "Momma's not gonna make me go now."

"Lito, you have 3 minutes to find your shoes, or you are walking to school barefoot in the snow."

Three minutes flew by, and I heard our front door open. I looked out of my bedroom, and saw momma standing at the front door, holding it open. She had to be bluffing. There was no way a she would make me go to school without shoes, especially not in the snow, would she?

"Get to walking. I'll see you after school," she said.

"But momma, I can't walk without my shoes."

"I don't know what to tell you! Get to school, now!"

I couldn't believe it. I put on my jacket, and walked out of the house.

"Have a nice day," mom said, then closed the door.

I stood at the bottom of the stairs of our front porch, and stared back at the front door. "No way!" I said. "She ain't right!"

After realizing that she was not going to change her mind, and after my feet started getting cold from standing in place, I started walking to school, barefoot, in the snow. As I walked away, I kept looking back at the trailer to see if mom was watching me. She wasn't. I walked very slowly hoping to hear her tell me to come back home. She didn't. The only thing I heard was the sound of ice crunching under my feet as I walked to school.

I walked about four blocks in the snow, and my feet, surprisingly, were just cold, but not freezing. I, however, was fuming. "How could momma be so mean? Why would she make me walk to school in the snow? Forget her!" I teetered between disbelief and anger all the way to school.

I turned left on Ursula street, and crossed a narrow dirt walkway to Vaughn, and walked along the chain-link fence to the entrance of the school. Then I stopped, there at the entrance. "Am I really going to do this? Am I really going to walk into school without shoes or socks on my feet?" It didn't take long for me to reach a conclusions. "No way! I ain't goin' to school barefoot!" Mom won.

I turned around, and hurried home, walked through my front door, and found my shoes. I called mom's bluff, and I lost. But the war had only just begun. That day I returned to school properly shoed, but mom's resolve did not do much to alleviate my disdain for school.

Realizing that mom would no longer give me permission to miss school, I had no other choice but to skip school behind her back. I began developing a talent for skipping school. That talent owed its existence to that cold winter day I walked to school barefoot.

So, about a week after the lost shoe episode, I came up with another way to avoid going to school. I was determined to miss school by any means necessary, and I thought I had found a way to do so without getting caught.

During that season of our lives, momma often stayed in her bed in the mornings while my brothers and I got ready for school by ourselves. Usually, because we all shared one bathroom, I stayed in bed a little longer than my brothers, so they could get ready first. Plus, their school, Central High School, was much farther away than Vaughn, so I didn't need as much time to get ready as they did.

So one morning, Juan or Jose turned on the bedroom light, and the brightness woke me up. I kept my eyes closed, acting like I was still asleep.

"Eeto, it's time to wake up, bud. You're gonna be late for school," Jose said.

"Okay, I'm up."

"Don't be late, bud. You know how mom gets."

"Okay, I'm up. I'm going."

Jose walked out of the room, out the front door, and then closed it. My brothers were headed to school.

"They're gone," I thought.

After they left, I acted like I was busy getting ready for school. I went to the bathroom, brushed my teeth, put on my clothes, my shoes, and my jacket. I opened the front door, then slammed the door from the inside, a little more loudly than usual.

Then I tiptoed back to my bedroom, closed the door, and went into my closet. I climbed into the tall stack of dirty clothes that were now five feet high, and I buried myself in the clothes. I covered my legs, my torso, and my head, only leaving a little whole through which I could breathe. I then balled some of the clothes into a pillow, and I laid my head down, and went to sleep.

I stayed under those dirty clothes for the entire day, from seven-thirty in the morning until three or four in the afternoon. I didn't eat, I didn't pee, I didn't move.

When my brothers got home at about three-thirty in the afternoon, I was still under that pile of dirty clothes. I waited quietly, listening for the right time to come out.

When I heard mom go into the bathroom and close the door, I knew that was my chance. So I snuck out the bedroom, and hurried out the front door, and went outside to play for a while. The first thing I did was go behind our trailer to relieve myself. I had been holding it all day, and I felt like my bladder was going to burst like a water balloon. Then, I went inside, greeted momma, acting like everything was normal.

"Hi momma! How was your day?"

"Hey baby! It was good," she replied. "How was your day?" She looked like everything was fine, like she had no idea I had missed school.

"How was school today?" she asked.

"It was good. I learned a lot," I said quickly, then changed the subject. "I gotta use the bathroom real quick momma. Then I jogged to the bathroom, and quietly filled the toothbrush cup up with water, and slowly poured it into the toilet so that it would sound like I was really going to the bathroom.

When I came out of the bathroom, I started heading toward the front door when mom asked me a question.

"Lito." I looked at mom, and she was looking at me, but she wasn't blinking. She continued, "is there anything you need to tell me?"

I blinked rapidly, and felt my breaths quicken. I looked at the doorknob, then at mom. "No, momma. I'm okay."

She tilted her head. "Are you sure?"

"How much did momma really know," I wondered.

13

I sensed mom was suspicious of something, but I certainly wasn't going to let her know that I had ditched school.

"Naw, momma. I'm good. Everything is okay. Everything that I can think of."

"Lito, are you sure you are not keeping something from me? You can tell me the truth." Her question felt like it had some damning evidence behind it.

I put my shaking hands in my pockets, and stuck to my guns. "Naw, momma. You got me nervous, like I did something wrong. I didn't do nothin momma. I promise."

"Well, your school called me today, and told me that you were not there today. Where were you today, Lito?" She crossed her arms and lowered her head and stared me in the eyes.

"They're lying momma. I was there."

"Then why would they call me and tell me you weren't there? That doesn't make any sense, does it? Are they making it up? Maybe we should just go down there right now and clear this up," she bluffed.

The hair on my body stood up because I knew I had been caught in a lie. I stuttered something, confessing that I had missed school.

"Lito, you need to go to school. I am very disappointed in you. You missed school and you lied to me about it. You are on punishment. You can't go outside, you can't play with your friends, and no watching t.v. Go to your room!"

I rushed to my room before she added to the punishment by pulling out her belt.

I laid there, on my bed for the rest of the night wondering how I had gotten caught. I realized that if I were going to get out of going to school that I was going to have to come up with something much more sophisticated. "I need to find a way to intercept the phone calls that come to our house, or else I'll keep getting caught." I laid on my bed strategizing, because I was determined to avoid school by any means necessary. I just could not bear being humiliated anymore. I would rather get a spanking, or put on punishment, than be embarrassed in front of my classmates again," I resolved.

While I linked pain to school, I linked a lot of pleasure to video games. When my third-grade classmate boasted about how his parents bought him a Nintendo and several video games, I envied him. I wanted to play video games too, but whenever I asked momma for video games, she often told me that we didn't have the money for them. So, I figured I would do whatever I had to do to get video games on my own.

That desire gave birth to my proclivity for shoplifting. I started stealing video games from stores. I actually became very good at it. I learned how to remove the security boxes, and the alarm sensors from the games so that I could exit the stores without setting off the alarms.

I blabbed to my cousin, Miguel, about it one day, and he wanted in.

"Lito, I want to go. Take me with you."

"Naw, Miguel, I don't want you to get caught."

"I promise I won't. If you show me how to do it, I promise I won't get caught, bud. Please take me with you."

"Okay, but only if you do exactly what I tell you to do."

A big smile came across his face. "Yeah! I'm about to get hooked up!"

We hopped on our bikes, and rode all the way to the store. We parked our bikes in the bike rack. Miguel started locking up his bike with a padlock.

"What are you doing, Miguel? No! Don't lock up your bike. We need to be able to take off right after we come out. We won't have time to unlock our bikes. You're gonna get us caught."

He looked so freakin' nervous. "Okay. My bad."

"Okay, let's go inside. Now remember. Do everything I tell you to do."

"I'm good, bud. Let's do this," he said.

We walked through the front doors. And I went through my usual routine: I walked over to the video game section, where all the electronics were, and I began scanning all the games. I grabbed about four of them, and turned to Miguel. "Grab one or two that you want, Miguel."

His eyes were big, and filled with fear.

"Calm down, Miguel. Don't look so scared. You're gonna get us busted!" I then walked away. I didn't want to stand next to him. He looked way too suspicious. I had a really bad feeling in my gut that things were not going to go well for me that day. But my greed got the best of me and I went against my instincts, and commenced to remove the packaging from the video games.

Miguel followed me to another aisle, and I quickly coached him. "Miguel, take the wrapper off the game, then pull the game out of the box, but be super quiet." I demonstrated it for him in a matter of three or four seconds.

Then I continued my lesson, "then you tuck it in your underwear like this." I lifted up my shirt, and tucked the game in the back of my pants, into the rim of my underwear.

"Put one in the front, and one in the back, if you're gonna get two," I instructed.

He was sweating profusely.

"Miguel, we're gonna be okay, but you gotta be fast, okay? Now go to another aisle and do what you gotta do, fast!" Then I walked away to spy the area to make sure no employees or security guards were around. It was clear. I opened the other three games and stuffed them in the front and back of my underwear, and started heading toward the exit. I walked passed the aisle Miguel was in, and he didn't have anything in his hands.

I asked him, "You good?"

He gave me a nervous nod.

My gut said something was wrong, but I didn't listen to it. We gotta go. So I said to him, "Good. Let's go. Wait ten seconds, then walk out of the aisle behind me, and go out the front doors, and meet me at our bikes. Okay?" I looked Miguel in his eyes, and he looked like he was gonna pass out.

"Fix your face, man! You're gonna get us caught!" I balled up my fists, threatening to hit him if he didn't get it together.

"I'm scared, bud," he said.

"Did you do what I told you to do?"

"Yeah."

"Then fix your face, and let's go! Be cool! Wait ten seconds, then come out behind me."

"Okay."

I walked away, and he counted to three and then came out of the aisle. He was walking like ten feet behind me.

"Oh well, I gotta just go with it now."

I got to the exit first, and walked through the alarm bars, and nothing happened. I made it out the doors and walked toward our bikes.

Then the store alarms went off behind me. I looked back and I saw Miguel standing there between the alarms.

I yelled at him, "Run, Miguel! Let's go! Run! Run! Run!" and I took off running full speed.

Then I heard Miguel yell for me, "Lito!"

I looked back, and he still hadn't come out of the store. He was frozen in fear, standing still at the door. A police officer ran up to Miguel and grabbed him by the arm.

He yelled again, "Lito!"

"No!!!!" I hollered. Should I keep running and get away, and have to explain to my family that I left Miguel by himself with the cops; or do I have to go back into the store and get arrested with him, and get taken to jail?

14

Standing outside that store, when Miguel called out my name the second time, I knew he had been caught. I got chills, and my stomach was rolling. My hands were trembling, and I was sprinting toward my bike. "No, no, no, no! This wasn't supposed to happen!" I thought to myself. "He didn't take the games out of the box like I told him!"

My heart was racing. "What am I gonna tell the family if I leave him here? What is gonna happen to me if I go back in there? I'm going to jail! I can't go to jail! I don't wanna go to jail."

I stopped running and just stood there for a second, staring at the door. I felt my pulse in my throat.

Then I walked back into the store, and saw Miguel crying, as he was being apprehended by a security guard. I walked toward them, and turned myself in, "It's okay, Miguel."

The security guard grabbed me, and yanked me by my arm. He then walked behind us, guiding us with his hand on the back of our necks, toward the holding room.

During our walk, Miguel kept crying.

I just stared at him, pissed off that he didn't run.

The security guard sat us in a small room, then called the cops.

"Empty your pockets," the security guard demanded.

Both Miguel and I lifted our shirts and pulled out all of the games we had hidden in the rim of our drawers. Sure enough, Miguel's games still had the plastic over them.

"Why are you guys up here trying steal games?"

We sat there silently, because there was no good answer.

"Okay, well if you guys don't want to talk to me, maybe you'll be more cooperative when the police get here." He stood up and walked out of the room, and on his way out, he said, "I'll be right back. Don't do anything stupid."

I looked at Miguel. He said, "I'm sorry Eeto! I messed up. I'm sorry!"

I roared, "Why didn't you run? We coulda got away! All you needed to do was run, Miguel!"

"I'm sorry, bud. I'm sorry. My legs froze. I was so scared, bud."

"Now we're gonna go to jail, Miguel. You should have ran!"

Then two cops walked into the room, and Miguel started crying again. "I don't wanna go to jail. I don't wanna go to jail. I'm sorry officer. I'm sorry. I don't wanna go to jail!"

"You should have thought of that before you came down here and tried to steal property that doesn't belong to you," the cop retorted.

"Now stop crying and stand up!" We both stood up.

"Turn around and put your hands behind your back. You are under arrest for shoplifting." They then put handcuffs on both of us. The cold metal of the cuffs clicked, and pressed up painfully against the bone in my wrists.

I stood there, looking down at the chair in front of me, playing the situation over and over in my head. I regretted my decision to bring Miguel with me. He didn't know any better, and I should not have taken him into that situation with me. It was all my fault. Now we were both going to jail.

I looked at Miguel, who was cuffed and still crying, and I said, "I'm sorry, Miguel. I shouldn't have brought you up here with me. My bad. We're gonna be okay, bud. We're gonna be okay."

I looked at the cops and said, "Please let my cousin go. It was my idea, and this was my fault. Please let him go home. Please officer."

I think they honored my request, because Miguel didn't have to go to court, and I was sentenced to some kind of "scared straight" program in which I had to sit with other young criminals and be threatened by police officers and former prisoners.

In that program, they made me stand up in front of the whole group and explain what I did to get arrested, and why I thought I made a stupid decision to shoplift. I think I lied and said something like, I would never steal again, or something like that. I'm pretty sure they were trying to teach me a lesson, but to be quite honest, I was convinced that the the most important thing I learned that day was that doing dirt with others only increased my chances of getting caught.

I got caught shoplifting during the first month of my fourth grade year at Vaughn elementary. Around that time, I think mom was longing for love and a little adventure in her life. Although she was about thirty years old, she had been raising kids since she was seventeen. So I think she wanted the chance to experience the freedom and excitement of life without taking care of kids. I think mom wanted her freedom back. So one day, she sat us down to tell us about an exciting opportunity that Doyle, her boyfriend, had presented to her. Although Doyle was in and out of the picture since I was five years old, neither my brothers nor I really knew who he was. I had seen him only a few times over a period of three or four years, but knew mom went out on dates with him on occasion.

She sat us down and said, "Guys, Doyle wants to take me to California for a little while."

My brothers and I all held still in expectation. "We might all be moving out there, but I need to go check it out first."

"Do we get to go with you?" I asked.

"Well, that's what I wanted to talk to you guys about. We don't have the money for all of us to go right now, but when I am able to save up enough, I am gonna to send for you guys, and we'll all be out there together. But first I gotta go see it."

My heart sunk because I didn't want to stay in Colorado alone. She could sense our reservations, and continued, "If I can only take one person on this trip, who would you guys want it to be?"

All three of us wanted to go with her.

"I wanna go with you, momma," I blurted out.

She lightly rubbed my arm, and with an understanding nod. "I know, baby. I wanna take all of you guys with me, but we just don't have the money right now. I can only take one of you guys on this first trip, but pretty soon, we'll all be together."

Juan offered his recommendation. "I think Jose should go, so he can look out for you mom, and me and Eeto will stay here. I'll take care of him."

Mom examined my face and then Julio's face to see what we thought. "I don't know. What do you guys think?"

"But we don't know anyone out there," Jose said.

"We'll have each other."

"Where will we stay?"

"Doyle has an apartment out there. We'll stay with him."

"What about school?"

"We'll find a school for you."

"How long would we be out there?" Jose asked.

"Not long. I was thinking maybe you could be out there a month or two, and then next month I can send for Juan and Lito."

The thought of being alone without momma for over a month terrified me. "But momma, who is gonna take care of us while you're gone?"

"Grandma will be next door. She'll cook for you and Juan, and make sure you guys are okay, and you and Juan will have each other."

"But momma, I don't want you to go. Why can't we all go together?" I pleaded.

"Lito, It's not gonna be long. Just a little while. Baby, pretty soon, all of us might be out there together."

"You're gonna come back and get us?"

"No!" she joked, but I didn't laugh. "What kind of mom do you think I am? You really think I'd go out there and leave you guys out here by yourself? Of course I'm gonna come back and get you guys!"

It was clear that mom's mind was made up; she was just trying to make sure we were okay with her decision. I was not comfortable with mom's decision, but knowing that I would have Juan with me made things a little better. Juan looked at me and said, "Bud, we're gonna be okay. We got each other's back." Then he looked at Jose, and ribbed him, "Bud, you're gonna go out there and see all those nice California chicks. Save some for me."

Mom smiled, got up and walked away.

Jose laughed, and responded, "Please, bud, I'm gonna go out there and be a big pimp." Then he leaned forward and whispered to us, "I'm gonna go out there and get some serious action." Juan and I both busted out laughing.

About a week later, mom and Jose packed their bags, and left for California. Juan and I just stood in the little driveway as they rode off in Doyle's black Trans Am. Once they turned at the end of the block, we looked at each other. Juan said, "Well, I guess it's just you and me, bud."

"I know, huh," I sighed.

We both walked up the stairs, into the trailer, and closed the door. I tried to act like I was okay for a while. "I gotta go to the bathroom." I got up and went into the bathroom, closed the door, turned on the sink, and sat on the toilet crying. Then, when I came out of the bathroom, I went to mom's room and laid down on her bed and cried some more. Momma and Jose hadn't been gone for ten minutes and I already missed them so much.

After a while, I guess there was one upside to mom being gone. I was free to do whatever I wanted: I stayed up late, watched all the television I wanted, and missed a lot of school. Furthermore, when I missed school, mom wasn't there to answer the phone when the school called; and, she wasn't there to see my terrible report cards in the mail.

It is indeed true that an idle mind is the devil's workshop, because while mom was in California, I formed habits that took me years to break.

15

After about two months of being in California, mom sent Jose back to Aurora, and made arrangements for me and Juan to join her. Neither Juan nor I really liked Doyle, because we didn't really know him. But the idea of going to California excited both of us. When he returned, Jose told us tales about the pretty girls, and the sandy beaches, and the warm weather.

"The weather is real nice. It's always sunny," he shared.

"What about the layyydiees?" I asked.

"They're fine too, bud. They're everywhere."

"We saw a picture of you at a concert," Juan said.

"Yeah, bud. They have concerts on the beach out there, and all the people come out and party. It's real cool. The people are cool too. Everyone is real chill."

It sounded really exciting, and Juan and I couldn't wait to see all those things for ourselves, especially the girls!

When Juan and I got to Long Beach, we moved into Doyle's studio apartment, which was right next to Franklin Middle School. The studio was small with a tiny kitchen and a small bathroom. Doyle, Mom, Juan, and I all lived in that tight space that couldn't have been more than five hundred square feet. Mom and Doyle slept on the pull-out couch, and Juan and I slept on the floor next to the bed.

Right across the street was a large home with huge yard and a tall orange tree. The only thing that separated me from the oranges was a medium-sized chain-link fence.

I snuck over that fence on more than one occasion to delight myself in the fruit of that tree.

Mom enrolled me in a school, but I hated it. It was already three or four months into the school year, so I was the "new kid from Colorado" at school. I walked into class that first day very timid and shy. I felt so out of place.

I remember the teacher talking about math, fractions or something, but I didn't understand anything he was talking about. It was painfully clear that I had fallen behind academically.

In that moment, the same feelings of inadequacy I felt in Mrs. Elliott's 3rd grade class flooded my mind. I didn't want to be there. I felt so alone. I sat alone in the cafeteria, because all the other kids had already formed their cliques. Sometimes I would get my food, put it in my pockets and then go outside to play just so I wouldn't have to eat alone. But even then, I couldn't find anyone to play with. I did not fit in anywhere, with anyone. The kids talked much faster, and their jokes were more crude, and their manner was more harsh.

Although Long Beach was only a thousand miles from Aurora, it felt like I was a million miles from home. I really felt like a stranger in a strange land.

My aversion to school expedited my return to a life of truancy. Instead of walking to school, I meandered through the streets of Long Beach. I was so nonchalant about missing school that I once walked into a pet store, in the middle of the day, at the Long Beach Mall and tried to buy a pet gerbil with a roll of quarters. But when the sales associate told me that I needed a parent's permission, I seriously argued with her.

When that didn't work, I marched my roll of quarters up the escalator to the mall's video arcade, where I had the whole place to myself, until an arcade employee confronted me. "Hey, little man. Why you out here?"

"I didn't have school today," I replied and kept playing my game.

"Man, today was not an off day at school. You gonna get in trouble if the cops see you in here."

"Why?"

"Cuz you supposed to be in school. They gonna come in here and take you to the truancy center across the street."

I didn't know what a truancy center was, but I was pretty sure I wanted no part of it.

"I gathered up my quarters and snuck out of the mall and walked around the city of Long Beach, all day, every day. I occasionally got chased by cop cars, but I learned to be pretty evasive.

Ditching school became a sport for me. I had to find ways to get food and not get caught. What I didn't know was that Juan had been ditching school too. I guess he had been having a hard time adjusting to Long Beach as well.

So one day, I decided that I was going to play hooky, and on our way out the door for school, I looked at Juan and said, "I'm not going to school today."

"Why bud?"

"Because I just don't like it."

"But bud, you have to go to school."

"Naw, I'm not going today."

He could tell I had made up my mind. "Well, I'm not going either, bud," he said.

"You been missing school too?"

"Yeah bud, I haven't been going either. I hate it out here in Long Beach."

I smiled because I now had a partner in crime.

"Cool, so where are we gonna go?"

"Let's go down to the beach. That's where I usually hang out."

So we started walking toward the beach. I was so excited to have my brother with me. Normally, I had ditched alone, but now I had a partner in crime.

We walked several blocks to the beach, and stopped in front of a hotel building. "We need to hide our books, bud." Juan walked behind a building, and saw some bushes. "Let's leave our bags here, and pick them up at the end of the day."

"Okay." We both tucked our books into the bushes making sure no one could see them, and then we jogged away. We jogged past a little white pickup truck at the corner, with a man sitting in the driver's seat. When he turned his head toward us, I looked away, acting like I didn't see him there. Plus, I didn't want to give him any indication that we had just dropped our books off in those bushes.

We walked along Ocean Boulevard for a while when we saw some stairs that went down to the beach. We started walking down the steps, and halfway down, we saw a homeless man sleeping on one of the benches that was halfway down the stairway. Juan and I looked at each other, smiled with devious looks in our eyes, and went back up to the top of the stairs.

"Let's throw something at him," Juan said.

I started getting giddy.

We both picked up some rocks, and gravel, and peanuts and some pennies, and whatever else we could find. Then we looked at each other to coordinate our throws.

"On the count of three," Juan said. "One…two… THREE." Our adrenaline was at full throttle when we hurled all the garbage at that homeless man. We jogged away laughing hysterically.

Seconds later, Juan hollered, "Run, Eeto! He's coming! Run, bud! Run!!!"

I turned around to see what Juan was screaming about, and I saw the homeless man barreling toward us. He was pissed off! He had spittle built up in the corners of his mouth, and his eyes were filled with fire. My eyes bulged out of my head, and my knees buckled.

16

With that homeless man running at us with sheer rage in his eyes, Juan and I ran into the street, into traffic. I was ahead of him. Tires screeched, horns honked. We kept running. Once I made it to the other side of the street, I looked back. The homeless man was crossing the street too. He was about 50 yards behind us. He was tall, black, slender, and fast. We sprinted a block, and turned right onto a street, hoping to lose him. But we looked back, and that man was running full speed and showing no signs of slowing down.

I was out of breath. My legs were getting tired. I couldn't run anymore. I bent over, hands on knees, wheezing, and crying. The homeless man was about to come around the corner at any moment, and catch me, because I could not run anymore. But Juan snatched me up, cradling me in his arms, and carried me to the back of a small brown building, then he put me down.

"Shhhh, Eeto." he whispered, putting his pointer finger to his lips, with fear and a sure strength in his eyes.

I just stood there, shaking, rolling stomach, feeling like we were about to die.

"Crap! He's coming down this street, bud," Juan said helplessly. "Get ready to run, bud."

I knew I didn't have much more in me. "He's gonna kill me. Oh god. Oh god. Oh god…" I looked around, and there was nowhere else to go.

As I sat there it total terror, Juan backed into me, turned around, eyes wide, and mouthed "He's right there bud. Don't move." He put his fingers over his lips again, to ensure my silence. I guess I may have been whimpering.

So I held my breath. The homeless man sprinted by, and I stood there, shaking…

When we finally came out from behind that building, Juan and I began walking down the street as if everything was okay. But that little white pick-up truck that I had seen earlier near our book-drop drove by us, and parked at the end of the block.

"Slow down, bud. There's someone in the truck. It might be him," Juan said.

"Let's turn around. Let's turn around," I urged, because I felt something was wrong. What were the chances that that was the same white pick-up truck I had earlier seen? So we kept walking.

As we were walking toward the corner, and closer to the truck, we were trying to look through the truck's back window, to get a better look at the driver. From behind, he had straight, dark, curly hair. He looked like he was in his late thirties or early forties.

When we got next to the truck, I saw the man in the truck leering at us with black, beady eyes, and fondling himself.

Juan yanked me. "Run, bud!" We ran around the corner, into an alley, and hid behind some dumpsters, and waited. The truck drove by, and like mice chasing a cat, we snuck out of the alley, and ran in the opposite direction. We meandered through the alleys and backstreets of Long Beach for the rest of the day, trying to avoid any more problems.

Finally, when the end of the day came, we went to retrieve our books from the bushes, but they were gone! Someone had taken our books. We couldn't tell mom we lost our books, because we were supposed to be at school. How were we going to do our homework? Mom was going to have to buy me new books. We don't have any money like that! There was no way I could go to school without my books, or my homework, I reasoned. I was already behind in class. Without books, I was really going to fall behind!

After being chased by that homeless man, I began ditching school almost every day. I was gone for about two weeks when I decided to try to go back to class. However, once I walked into my class, the teacher told me that I needed a note from my doctor explaining why I had been out of school for so long. I couldn't get my mom to write me a note, and I knew no doctor would write a note for me. So, again, I missed another couple weeks before I tried to return to school again.

The school called the house, but no one was ever home. On several occasions, people would come by our house, and knock on the door. With nobody home but me, they often taped something to our doors. I waited until they left, and peeked through the sheer curtains to make sure they were gone. I opened the door, pulled the note off the door. The note said something like, "Dear Ms. Rose Sarmiento, Manuel Sarmiento has missed more than forty-five days of school this semester. Please contact us as soon as possible."

I knew I had messed up, but I didn't know how to fix things. Then, something happened to make school even less of a priority for me.

One night, mom and Doyle had gone out to party at a club while Juan and I stayed home alone. We never liked it when they went out because it usually meant trouble.

That night, it was late, and Juan and I were asleep on the floor when mom and Doyle came in the front door, and went into the bathroom. They were doing crack. After about 20 minutes, I heard them begin arguing. I heard mom denying something. Their voices got a little louder when I heard my mom telling Doyle to stop. Juan and I, both lying their on the floor listening, didn't say anything because we were not even supposed to be awake. Then we heard a loud slap, and heard mom scream. Doyle was calling her some terrible names, and he hit her again.

Unable to take it any longer, Juan and I jumped up, turned on the lights, and rushed to the bathroom door.

"Mom are you ok?" I asked. "Doyle, leave my mom alone! Let her out!" I continued.

"Go back to sleep. We're fine," Doyle said, brushing us off.

We turned the door knob, but the door was locked. We tried to pull it open, but it wouldn't move. Doyle hit mom again, and again, and she kept screaming. Juan and I were both standing at the door enraged.

Juan hollered out, "If you think you're bad, come and hit me like that!"

The door opened, I saw my mom bent over the sink, and her face was red, and blood was dripping from her mouth. Doyle rushed out, looked straight at Juan and said, "you don't want none of me."

My brother was scared, but he had no choice. Although he was barely fourteen at the time, Juan did his best to protect momma. Doyle and my brother squared up. My brother grabbed Doyle, and Doyle slammed him against the wall. Juan tried to push Doyle, but he was just too strong. He picked my brother up, and again slammed him against the wall. Doyle body slammed Juan onto the floor, and my brother just wouldn't give up.

Mom was screaming for Doyle to stop, but he wouldn't. Crying, I rushed to the phone, and called 911. While while I was on the phone, trying to get help, I looked over and saw my brother getting choked. I jumped on Doyle's back, and tried to choke him from behind.

Juan got out of his grip, and screaming in total rage, rushed Doyle again. Doyle, too strong for my brother, grabbed Juan again, and threw him up against the wall, and slid him across the wall until Juan fell to the floor and just laid there. Mom was screaming. I ran to him to see if he was okay. He was bleeding from his mouth, and had scratches on his neck.

My brother was just too young to be fighting a grown man.

Doyle got up, looked at me. I was standing there, with my fists balled up, looking him in his eyes, with hatred. He challenged me, "boy, when you think you bad enough. You let me know." He walked out the front door, slammed it. We heard him start his black trans-am, and peel off.

Juan was in the bathroom mirror with blood in his mouth and scratches on his neck and back. My mom was crying, and she was trying to tend to Juan, and I was there with both of them in the bathroom, sitting on the edge of the tub. Just watching. Scared. Confused. Angry. Relieved that was all over, for now.

17

The next morning, after getting a few hours of sleep, the phone rang. Mom picked it up. The tone of mom's voice told us it was Doyle. I just knew he was calling to apologize for the night before. I thought to myself, "No grown man should ever put his hands on a woman or a child. He has to be on the phone begging mom for her forgiveness." My young mind just knew Doyle had realized the error of his ways, and wanted to somehow tell us how sorry he was for the monster he had become the night before.

Mom walked into the kitchen for a little privacy, so Juan and I took the cue. We got up and went to the bathroom. I got in the shower, and Juan brushed his teeth and got dressed. While I was showering, I could still see some of mom's blood on the edge of the tub.

After I came out of the bathroom, I noticed mom was angry. She was pacing, and cussing.

"What's wrong, momma?" I asked.

"Doyle has kicked us out…we have until 3pm to get out." I couldn't believe it. We didn't have any family in Long Beach. All our people were in Colorado. We didn't have any money and mom didn't have a job.

"Where are we going to go, momma?"

Trying not to reveal her own uncertainty and fear, mom just said, "c'mon, Juan, Lito, grab all the things that you need."

Mom filled her suitcase with clothes, so Juan and I started filling our suitcases with clothes too.

Mom turned Doyle's Hinkley Springs jug, which was filled with coins and cash, upside down, and took all the green and silver we could find.

We walked to the beach- the same beach where Juan and I threw gravel at the homeless man. We walked down the same steps, passed the same bench on which he was sleeping, to the beach so we could sit there, and give mom a chance to figure out what were were going to do.

We settled in a secluded spot on the beach. Mom told us to wait there while she made some calls on the pay phone. We really had nowhere to go. And we had absolutely no family or friends we could call for help. As I sat there, looking out at the water, in silence, it was like I could hear my conscience saying, "being homeless ain't so funny now, is it?"

Mom opened the yellow pages that were attached to the phone booth, and began skimming through pages. I had no idea what she was looking for, but I could tell she found something. She took the phone off the hook, put in her two dimes (and a quarter), and dialed a number. She started talking to someone. Cradling the phone between her right shoulder and right ear, she scribbled notes on the back page of the phone book. Mom hung up and dialed another number. Mom made several calls while Juan and I sat there hoping that mom would figure something out. After an hour, mom walked back over to us, and said she found a place where we could stay that night. To be honest, any place was better than the streets or the beach.

We stayed the night at an old, run-down motel. Once we walked past the caged clerk's desk, we went up some rickety, winding stairs. They creaked, and reeked of urine, cigarette smoke, and must. The hallway lights were flickering. But they were bright enough for us to see our room number in spurts. Mom put her key in the door while Juan and I looked around at the stained carpet, marked walls, the chipped wall-paper. It felt like we were in some horror movie or something. Like someone was watching us.

Mom opened the door, turned on the lights, and we rushed in, closing the door behind us. The room was small, with really old, green, peeling wall paper. Peeking through the green wallpaper was the pink, yellow, and brown layers of paint that looked like it had been there for at least a hundred years. The heater was one of those old metal wall heaters. The bed was a full size mattress with an old brown wooden headboard. The room was so small that there was barely room to walk. There were maybe a couple of feet of space in between the walls and the mattress. There was a little more space at the foot of the bed and the dresser that had a small, old T.V. on it.

I untied my shoes, and jumped into the bed. I rolled over onto my back, right in the center of the bed, and rested my head on the pillow. My feet were sore from all that walking. I then scooted to the edge of the bed and looked out the window. I saw drug dealers on the corners. There were women in prostitution too. One of them caught me looking, and that was enough for me to close the curtains.

Juan took off his shoes, and crawled onto the bed with me and mom. Mom pulled out the generic bread and bologna, and we ate dinner. We used our hands as cups to drink water from the bathroom sink.

I turned on the T.V., and got back on the bed. As bad as the room was, with its odors, and ugly wallpaper, and bedbugs, and roaches- it was still better than the beach we almost had to sleep on.

We lived like that, in motels, an shelters, and at strangers' houses until mom ran out of money. One day, while we were roaming the streets, I could tell that momma didn't feel so well. She was moving more slowly, and needing to take more rest breaks.

We could tell she was not at herself, and convinced her to visit the free neighborhood clinic. We waited a long time for the doctor to see mom. Juan and I sat in the waiting room while mom went in to get checked out. We just stared at the doctor's closed door, hoping mom was okay.

When mom walked out, she looked at us and just said, "let's go." We could tell something was wrong, but didn't want to do anything to make her any more uncomfortable. So we just walked behind mom in silence.

While walking to the park where we usually sat, with the rest of the homeless folks of Long Beach, we asked her what was wrong with her. She insisted that she was fine. During the course of the day, on several occasions, mom got dizzy and needed to sit down. We broached the subject of her health again, and asked what was wrong. "Momma, you can tell us. What did the doctor say?"

She hesitated for a moment, then looked up at us, and said, "The doctor told me I have tuberculosis, and that I'm four months pregnant." My jaw dropped in disbelief. I didn't know what tuberculosis was, but it sounded like something that was going to take my mom away from me. And pregnant?

I remember feeling scared and a deep desire to be of more help to my mom. I wanted to make life easier for her, but, in reality, I was just a boy, and I couldn't even take care of myself. How could I take of momma?

Juan just sat there in silence. He looked just as concerned as I did.

One day, we walked all over Long Beach looking for a place to sleep. It felt like we had walked over ten to fifteen miles. But every place we looked into was full. They couldn't fit any more people. I wondered what we were gonna do. We were still hungry even though we had just eaten soup from a soup line a little earlier in the day. My stomach was growling, it was getting late and cold outside. I was getting a little nervous. I worried that we were going to have to sleep on the streets.

We stopped by the Long Beach Rescue Mission, and, we saw a long line of people who, like us, were hoping to get in. A guy gave us permission to sleep on the floor in the main area with everyone else.

We walked into this small room, the lights were dimmed, and people were laid out all over the place. All of the corners were occupied, and all of the spaces next to the walls were taken. We found a small open space near the center of the room, maybe the size of a twin bed, and we sat down on the the floor. It was concrete. It was very cold.

Scanning the room, I saw a lot of people who looked like life had beaten them up. Wrinkles filled with dirt, and sunken, despondent eyes were everywhere I looked. For those who still had their heads up high enough, I could see sadness in their eyes. Most of the people in the room were men, but there were some women as well. Most of them seemed familiar with those sleeping arrangements. While there were some folks there who looked like pedophiles, rapists, and murderers, most of the people in that room looked like normal, everyday people who had just fallen on hard times, like us.

I was starving. A man walked around with a white bag filled with white and wheat bread rolls. He went to each person and with a white rubber glove on his hands, he handed out a piece of bread to each person who wanted one. They gave me, Juan, and mom a piece of brown bread.

Mom handed me her bread, "here, eat this."

I asked, concerned, "mom, aren't you hungry?"

"No, Lito. I'm okay," she said. "You and Juan split this."

I felt as though mom was not telling the truth, but I was so hungry that I didn't argue with her. I took the piece of bread, took off my jacket, rolled it up, put it under my head, and used it as a pillow. I laid there on that floor, on my side, holding that piece of bread, and tears began to roll off my nose onto my jacket. We had no blankets, no pillows, no beds, no money. Just a piece of bread.

Questions ran through my head, like, "Why are we here?" "How could Doyle kick us out like this?" "What kind of man does that?" The questions quickly turned to conclusions: "I hate him." "I will never be a man like that."

Mom saw my tears, took off her jacket, and laid it over the top of me. Holding back her own tears, with a determination in her eyes, she assured me that everything was going to be okay. I remember her saying, "Mijo. we're going to be okay."

As much as I wanted to believe mom, everything about our situation told me that we were not anywhere near okay.

We bounced from shelter to shelter, and I had days when I was incredibly hungry. I could not go to school to eat because I needed a note from a doctor to justify why I had been absent from school for over 2 months. So I had not been eating breakfast or lunch. All I remember eating for dinner most days was a small bowl of soup and a piece of bread. There were days when I was just starving. Mom thought I was going to school, and eating at school, but I wasn't.

One day I was walking by a McDonald's, and I was so hungry that I went inside and just stared at the people buying food. They got their food, and sat down at the tables, and ate. I sat there hoping they would leave some fries, or one of their hamburgers on the table, but most people devoured their food.

One guy left half of his cheeseburger unfinished. I was hoping he would just leave his tray on the table and leave. Instead, he took it to the trash. It took everything in me to not go stick my hand in that trash can to grab that cheeseburger, but I was too embarrassed by what other people would think about me.

I hoped someone would see me, and offer to buy me a Happy Meal or something, but everyone avoided eye contact with me. It was incredible how invisible I became to most people.

Sometimes I would sit in, or near, a restaurant until it was about to close so I could see what the managers were going to do with their leftover, unsold food. I figured they had to throw the food in the garbage every night, or at least that was my hope.

So I often went outside the restaurant, near the drive-through, which was right next to a dumpster, and I hid in some nearby bushes. I didn't want anyone to see what I was about to do. There were still several cars in the drive through. I was hoping they didn't order any of the hamburgers I had just seen inside. The last car was served, the restaurant lights turned off, and I waited eagerly in the those bushes.

About an hour went by when the restaurant's back door opened, and I saw an employee carrying a couple large, black garbage bags in his hands. He opened the fence where the dumpster was housed, he lifted the lid, and he threw both bags in. My heart started to beat. I couldn't wait to find those burgers in there. I waited until the last employee left, and I hurried over to the fence. I climbed it as quietly as I knew how, and I lifted the lid of the dumpster, and I jumped in and closed the lid on top of me. It was dark, but I felt around for the bags that were just dropped off. I was feeling each bag for warmth. I tore open several of the bags, and felt around for big mac boxes, but there were none. There were no cheeseburgers. There were only empty cups, with ice, unfinished drinks, and some fries. I ate as many of the fries as I could find, but they were stale, very hard, and pretty disgusting. But I was so hungry...

After I finished eating, I peeked my head out of the dumpster to make sure no one was around, and I quickly jumped out, over the fence, and walked home.

It is hard to put into words what experiences like that did to my psyche- the shame, and degradation that seeped into my soul is inexpressible. While I was doing what I had to do to survive, there was part of my soul that was becoming calloused.

Shortly thereafter, mom got us into a homeless shelter, where we lived for about a month or two while she saved up enough money to buy us plane tickets to Colorado. We finally made it home. However, while things were bad in Long Beach, they became much worse when we returned to Colorado.

18

Back in Aurora, we moved in with aunt Molly for about a month until we got back on our feet. Then we moved into the Del Mar Apartments, a housing complex that was pretty much the equivalent of projects. Nonetheless, I was relieved to have a place of our own again, and I was determined to get back into school. To be quite honest, I was grateful for a chance to turn over a new leaf. I no longer needed a doctor's note to get back into school; all I had to do was show up. That was great, mostly because I could go back to eating at school.

I enrolled in Lynn Knoll Elementary, where I was placed in Miss. Dreezen's 4th grade class. It was the spring semester, and there were a few months of school left in the year. In class, I payed attention, but, as usual, I kept to myself. The school day was over, and she told the class what homework we needed to have finished. I was determined to start off on the right foot.

I got home, and sat down at the coffee table to begin working on my homework. I worked through the basic addition problems. The subtraction problems. The multiplication problems. They took me some time, but I was doing my best, and doing okay. However, when I started working on an assignment that contained fractions, I got stuck. I just didn't understand them. I needed help. I went to the bedroom to ask my mom to help me with with my fractions, but being six months pregnant, she was lying in her bed, watching t.v.

She told me to go figure it out. I stomped out of her room, and walked to the kitchen to see if there was anything to eat.

On the counter were several little round, flaky rock-looking things. I didn't know what they were. I picked one up. I examined it, smelling it and tasting it. It tasted salty! It was rock cocaine. Mom walked into the kitchen and told me not to touch them. I remember saying to myself, "she can't help me with my fractions, but she has time to divide that crack on the counter."

I went back to the coffee table, and looked at my homework for a couple more minutes. But I was just not that interested in it anymore. Mom left the kitchen and went back into her bedroom and closed the door.

"Forget this!" I said in frustration. "If she doesn't care about my homework; why should I?" I got up and went outside, and found something else to get into.

A few months later, my little brother, Noah, was born. He was a beautiful little guy. I used to spend hours with him, playing with him, and feeding him, and doing all the things that big brothers do with their new baby brothers. That little guy brought me so much joy. I hoped that with his arrival, things would begin to get better for us as a family. Unfortunately, that didn't happen.

One night I came home to what felt like an empty house. I wondered, "Where is everyone?" I went into my bedroom, and I saw Noah asleep on the bed. "Maybe mom is asleep too," I guessed. So I walked into her room, and I'll never forget what I saw- the lights were off, but I let enough light into the room by opening the door that I could clearly see a room full of people looking directly at me. The room was filled with smoke, and their eyes were vacant. I was scared. It felt like I walked into a room filled with demons. There was a very black, sinister energy in the room.

Doyle was in the room too. Confusion flooded my mind. They were smoking crack. My mom hollered at me to close the door. But her voice was different. She yelled like she didn't even know me. It was scary because the woman I called "mom" was clearly not my mom. She was someone else. Possessed by a spirit that was devoid of love. I quickly closed the door and rushed to the kitchen, and grabbed a large knife, hid it under my shirt, and rushed back to my bedroom with my little brother.

I was scared, and wanted to leave to find Juan and Jose, but I couldn't leave my little brother alone in that house with those monsters. So I sat there in the dark, watching the shadows pass my door. "What are they doing? And why is Doyle here? He better not come in here! Forget him, after all he did to us!" I laid down on the bed, next to my baby brother, hoping to comfort him, but in actuality, I think his little frame comforted me.

19

The day after I saw everyone smoking crack in mom's bedroom, I walked into my living room. Mom was sitting on the couch watching T.V. As a ten year old boy, I didn't know how to broach the subject of what I had seen the night before, but I wanted- needed- to know why Doyle was at our house, "Momma, what was Doyle doing here last night?"

"I know, Lito," was all she said, almost ashamed, acknowledging how absurd it was for him to be there.

I needed more than acknowledgement though. I couldn't let it go, "Momma, he hurt you. He hurt Juan; he hurt all of us. He kicked us out on the streets, and you were pregnant. We were homeless momma. We slept on floors."

"I know, Lito. I know... but Doyle loves me, mijo."

"No! No! Why would you let him- Him!- back into our lives?"

She just stared at me, and my rage bubbled. Before I knew it, I blurted out, "You're stupid!"

I guess part of my anger was from the fact that Doyle never, not once, ever, said sorry for the way he treated me, my brothers, or my mom. So, in my heart, all I could feel as a ten-year-old child was hatred. I made it clear to mom that I didn't want to be there when he came around; that I didn't want anything to do with him.

All she could say, again, was, "It's going to be okay. Doyle loves me. We'll be okay."

When Juan and Jose found out about Doyle, they were outraged. Especially Jose, because he had heard about what Doyle did to us. So whenever Doyle came around, my brothers and I often went outside. We didn't speak to him. We wanted nothing to do with him.

But the inevitable clash between Doyle and our resentment finally made its way to our living room one night, when Doyle and my brothers got into it. I don't remember the exact incident that prompted the argument, but it really could have been about anything, because the fight was really rooted in the bitterness we had toward him.

"You punk!" Jose hollered at Doyle.

Doyle dared Jose and Juan to try something, "I'll kick both of your behinds."

Juan and Jose stood up to take up Doyle's offer; he stood up too. Mom jumped in, and urged everyone to calm down. But emotionally, my brothers were teetering on the edge of the point of no return, and had mom not stepped in, Doyle would have probably been killed that night.

Mom told my brothers to go for a walk, but my brothers couldn't resist asking the obvious, "Mom, why are you picking him over us? After what he did to you and us?" You could hear the pain in their voices. They continued, "Why? Why do you keep picking him over us?"

I cried when my brothers moved back to Sterling the next day. I really wanted to leave with my brothers, but I didn't want to leave my mom alone with Doyle. I didn't trust him.

Shortly after my brothers left, mom and Doyle went out to the club while I babysat Noah, who was asleep in mom's bed. As I usually did when mom and Doyle went out, I reclined on the living room couch, and watched T.V. I stayed up, flipping through channels until about 2 in the morning, when I heard some commotion outside the front door of our apartment, in the hallway. I turned down the T.V. Being stealth was important because if the police found me or Noah home alone, they would take us away from mom. So I needed to stay very quiet. Mom instructed, "If anyone knocks on the door, take Noah, and hide somewhere, and stay super quiet until they leave."

Well, that night, I followed the guidelines. Lights off, T.V. off, and I snuck to the bedroom where Noah was asleep, and I listened. I heard a scream. I quietly hurried to the door, and put my ear to the door to hear what was going on. It sounded like the neighbors were fighting. As mom and I always did for entertainment, we would put a glass to the door to try to amplify what they were saying. With my ear against the door, I heard a man's voice. It sounded like Doyle. I hoped it wasn't.

Then I heard my mom beg, "Stop, you're hurting me. You are hurting me. Doyle, let go."

My stomach tightened.

"Help!" Mom whimpered. Then she called my name. "Lito! Lito! Help me! Somebody help me! Call the police! Somebody call the police! You're hurting me, Doyle!"

I picked up the phone and dialed 911. I told them that a man was hurting my mom and she needed help. "She's in the hallway, screaming for help. Please come and help my momma! Please come and help my momma! Please!" I begged.

I heard the sound of crashing glass, and mom let out the most helpless, heart wrenching scream I'd ever heard. In a panic, I hung up the phone, and rushed to the door. I opened it, ran out, smelled liquor and saw blood. Doyle was standing behind my mom, and he was holding her by the back of her head, by her hair. He was holding her by her left arm so she couldn't get away. Blood was all over momma's neck, drenching her collar and bleeding down through her blouse. It became immediately clear to me that Doyle had just slammed mom's head through the large glass window that was in our apartment building's hallway. Momma was screaming frantically, "Lito, help me! Help me!"

Scared to death, I ran up behind Doyle, punched him in his back as hard as I could, and then jumped on his back. I hardly inflicted any damage on him, but I did my best. It was just enough to cause him to let go of my mom. But before he could grab me, I jumped off his back and ran. He turned around and rushed toward me. I sprinted back into the apartment, but I had nowhere to go! He ran in behind me, hollering. I was cornered.

We lived on the second floor, so the only way of escape was to go out to the balcony. He lunged toward me with rage in his blood-shot eyes, with his teeth gritted, and his brow creased. I was terrified. I tried to climb over the rail to slide down the pole, but he was coming too fast. He grabbed my shirt, and tried to pull me back over the railing, but I wiggled free from his grip, and fell two stories off the balcony, scraping my ribs on a bolt on the way down. I landed on my back, and laid there, dazed.

When I looked up at the balcony, Doyle was gone. I feared he was rushing down the stairs to get me, so I got up, and took off running toward the street, looking in every direction for some sign that help was on the way.

While I couldn't see any cop cars, I heard their sirens, which sounded like they were a few minutes away. I looked back and saw Doyle come out of the building. He jumped in his black Trans-Am, and screeched off.

I ran back into the apartment building looking for momma. I saw blood from the window, on the rail, on the carpet, and there was a trail of blood leading back into the front door of our apartment. I searched feverishly for my mom. I heard Noah crying. He was still in mom's bedroom. I saw a trail of blood leading to the bathroom. I ran to the entrance of the bathroom door, and mom was on the floor. There was blood all over the sink. She was pressing a towel over her neck and the side of her face. Blood was soaking through the towel. And my mom was crying. I didn't know what to do. I felt so helpless.

The police and paramedics eventually arrived, and did whatever they had to do to make sure she was okay.

There were many nights like that one that I would rather not remember, but that stick with me. Nonetheless, those experiences made it very difficult to care about school.

One day, after a long night of mom and Doyle, and cops, and ambulances, I was sitting in class, both tired and sad. I felt so alone. Like no one really understood me. How could they? How many people in my classes were going through the things I lived with? How many teachers really knew anything about domestic violence or child abuse? What did they know about living in fear, being homeless, and surviving? I wondered.

So, I was sitting there during a class assignment, and my teacher was talking, about something. Her lips were moving, but I honestly didn't really hear her. Yes, sound was coming out of her mouth, but I just could not focus. No matter how hard I tried, I could not have cared less about what she saying. On my mind was mom's blood that was all over our bathroom. On my mind were mom's screams for help. The teacher was covering her content, but I was thinking about my sore ribs. The teacher kept talking, but I kept thinking about the fact that my brothers had just been arrested in Sterling for beating up some guy who called them "dirty Mexicans" or something. So I sat there, in class, unable to focus, because nothing that teacher was saying seemed relevant to all of the things that were going on in my life.

I started looking around at the other kids, and they were laughing. I guess the teacher had told the class that they could talk, or work in groups, because the kids were starting to move around. They were getting markers out, and paper out. I just sat there. I looked over at the kid sitting next to me, and noticed he had brand new shoes on his feet. Then I looked down at my feet, at the oversized, holy shoes with cardboard in them. I had to curl up my toes to keep the cardboard pressed down against the sole of the insides of my shoes so the cardboard would not slide, causing my sock to fall through the big, embarrassing holes that were in the soles of my shoes. I remember looking around the room, at the other shoes in the room, and some kids had on expensive Jordan's, or some nice, clean, new shoes. I just felt so ashamed.

I felt my heart asking, "Why is it that everyone else has nice shoes and nice clothes, and I have holes in my shoes? Why are my pants too big for me? Why does everyone else have nice back packs and lunch pales, but I don't have one? Why do I have a duffle bag and everyone else has a backpack? Why do all the other kids bring good food to school, but I don't?" The questions were humiliating.

The kids were laughing, having a good time, but I couldn't even find it in me to smile. I sat there numb. Calloused. Hardened.

"Why does everyone seem so happy, and I don't smile anymore? What's so funny? What is there to be happy about? I want to laugh too. Tell me a joke. I wanna laugh!" The contrast between me and those around me was enraging, "Ain't nothin' funny to me. I just saw my mom get punched in the face by a man. Tell me a joke, I wanna laugh. My brothers are locked up. Tell me something funny. I wanna laugh. I just fought a grown man last night, and I was forced off of a balcony, and my ribs are sore. What's so funny? I wanna laugh. Someone, please, tell me a joke. I wanna laugh too. Ain't nothin' funny!"

I felt really different from all the kids in my classes. But what really pushed me over the edge was a teacher. One day, I was sitting in class, wearing clothes that probably hadn't been washed in a month or two, and I was wearing those same old hand-me down shoes from my brothers, who were five years older than I was.

My sixth grade teacher asked a question. I was sitting next to one of the nephews of billionaire Charles Schwab- I think their names was Matthew or Michael. Why they attended my school, I'll never know. They had red hair and freckles.

My teacher asked the entire class a question about the homework assignment.

She wrote a few fractions on the board, and asked for volunteers to go to the board and complete them. Several kids raised their hands. I did not. But she called on me anyway. She asked, "why don't you give it a try?"

I shrunk in my chair.

She asked, "you did your homework last night, didn't you?"

I answered honestly. "No, ma'am. I tried, but I didn't understand it."

Then, in a very condescending tone, she asked, "*NOBODY* at home could help you with your homework?"

I felt terrible. "No, ma'am. They didn't understand it either."

She rolled her eyes. "Stand up," she said. Already feeling stupid for not understanding the homework, I stood up. Then she asked, "Why do your clothes look like that?"

Her question knocked the wind out of me. I just looked down at my shirt, and my raggedy pants, and my big shoes with the holes in them, then looked up at her. "Don't you have a washing machine at home?" she continued.

"No, ma'am," I said, shaking my head.

"Come with me," she ordered. She picked some other kids to go to the board, and told the class she would be right back. She took me out to the hallway, just outside her door, and said "your clothes stink…The kids in class are complaining that your clothes are stinking up the class."

The shame was so torturous that I couldn't say a word.

She continued, "Why do your clothes look like this? You don't have a washing machine at home?"

"No, ma'am," I said. Embarrassed was an understatement. As though she still had not heard, or understood, a word I had said, she then foretold my future,"if you don't get your act together, and start doing your homework, you are not going to graduate from school. You are going to probably go to prison, and you are probably going to end up just like your father. Isn't he in prison or something?" While she was probably right, she was wrong. Yes, given my circumstances, she was probably correct in predicting my future, but embarrassing me in front of the class, and then telling me that my clothes stunk, was certainly not the best way to win me over, or help me. Had I felt like she cared about me as a person, then maybe I would have been more receptive to what she said. Had she expressed more concern about why my clothes looked like that, or why my shoes had holes in them, or why I never did my homework, or why I always looked tired, then maybe, just maybe, she could have begun to understand how best to help me.

Instead, she looked at me through her white, midwestern, middle-class frame of reference, which believed that most families had their own washing machines, ate three healthy meals a day, and had parents that had the time and education to help their kids with homework. While her frame of reference was not inherently bad, it blinded her to the pain of my daily reality, and it caused her to be culturally and socioeconomically insensitive to kids who did not share her frame of reference.

But how could I, as a little boy, care about math and integers when my personal life was full of fractions and frictions? How could I care about helping verbs at school, when words never seemed to help me at home? How could I care about the different food groups the body needs to be healthy, when I barely had enough food at home to survive? How could I focus on schoolwork when defending my mother from a crack-addicted alcoholic became a regular part of my homework? And, how could I care about going to school when I wasn't even sure I would have a home to go to at night?

That teacher failed to understand that she didn't just teach reading, writing, or math; she taught reading *to kids*, she taught writing *to kids*, she taught math *to kids*; and, because she somehow forgot that basic truth, she made an already bad situation much worse for me.

So, while standing there, in front of that teacher, feeling pretty bad about myself, I looked up at her, and just said, "yes, ma'am."

That experience taught me that poverty is not only about lacking money; poverty is lacking access to the kinds of people who can help you make the most of your life. I concluded that those kind of people- people who wanted more for me, who believed in me, who would not harm me, who would help me become somebody- could not be found in my schools. So I decided then and there to no longer subject myself to that kind of pain and misery. My self-worth was so damaged that I could not bear even one more touch of humiliation. So, then and there, I decided I would do whatever I needed to do to miss school.

20

Because of everything that was going on at home and school, I started gravitating more toward my cousin Beto when I was about eleven years old.

Beto was older than me by a year or two. He was more advanced with the girls, and had more swagger than most people. He had always been cooler than I was. He had nicer clothes and nicer things than me. In a lot of ways, I wanted to be just like Beto.

One night, Beto was hanging with some guys, and he came by to pick me up. I hopped into the back seat of the car, and we drove for a while. In the car were two other people, but I don't remember who they were. We drove to a secluded area in the woods, and someone pulled out some weed, zig zag papers, and rolled a joint.

I was thinking, "crap! In school, they told us to 'Just Say No!' to drugs." The driver lit up the joint, took a hit, then passed it clockwise to Beto, who was sitting shotgun. He hit the joint, then passed it back to the person sitting behind him. He took a big hit, inhaling deeply, and then passed it to me. I didn't want to act like I didn't know what I was doing, and look like a lame. I hesitated for a quick second when my cousin looked back at me, and teased, "Hit it, don't babysit it!"

I let out a nervous laugh, and thought, "Forget it! You only live once! Don't be no punk!" I lifted the joint, put it to my lips, holding it between my left pointer finger and my thumb, and I inhaled deeply. Rather than easing into it, I took too big of a hit. The smoke entered my mouth, rushed into my lungs, and I lost it! I started coughing and choking! My eyes welled up with tears.

I passed the joint, and tried to regain my composure...

After about fifteen minutes of that, the windows fogged up, and had smoke filled the car. The smoke was so thick I could barely see. I started feeling really mellow. Really chill. Everyone was silent. We were high. I was eleven years old, and high.

21

After I started smoking weed at the age of 11, I also started breaking into houses. I got tired of seeing other people have a bunch of "extra," while me and my family had almost nothing. It was frustrating to see kids with two or three bikes and several pairs of new shoes, while me and my brothers had shoes with holes in them. It was even worse when kids who had a lot of material things made fun of us, who had very little. So, because I didn't have any money, the only logical thing for me, and many of us, to do was to start taking things from other people. That's why I started seriously stealing.

It started off with me stealing sodas from vending machines. Then I started stealing candy from convenience stores. Then I started stealing bikes from peoples homes and from schools. Then it turned into me stealing teachers' guides so I could improve my grades. Eventually it evolved into me stealing money from the purses of librarians and others.

As I started getting good at it, I started stealing groceries from supermarkets. Then I started breaking into post offices, and stealing credit cards, dog mace, and happy face stickers. Then I started stealing video games from bigger stores.

Eventually I started breaking into homes. Since I hadn't been going to school, I spent more time roaming the streets. There was a park in the neighborhood that I used play at (or at least act like I was playing at), and I would sit on the swings, sometimes all day, and observe people. I started noticing certain patterns. I noticed that every morning at the same time, certain people would get into their cars and drive off. I also noticed that people are creatures of habit, and they followed that routine like clockwork every day.

So one day, after observing a few homes for about a week, I watched people leave in the mornings, and I saw them return in the afternoon. I knew what time they left in the morning, and what time they would return. I knew what time they walked their dogs, and watered their grass.

So one day, I decided I was going to break into one of their houses. From a distance, on the swing, I watched the man and his significant other get into their cars and drive off. I waited about ten minutes, then walked nonchalantly to their home. I walked up their driveway, to their back yard. I jumped the fence, and noticed they had a little dog entrance. I was nervous, but went in anyway. I crawled quietly through the entrance, and looked for the little dog.

Sure enough, a dog ran into the kitchen and started barking loudly at me. Knowing that dogs can smell fear, I remained calm as best as I could even though I was terrified, and walked it to the back of the house, into the bathroom. He barked at me all the way through the house, but he didn't try to bite me. I led him into the bathroom. I then closed the door, and trapped him inside.

I was afraid that the dog's loud bark had alarmed some of the neighbors, so I peeked out the windows to see if anyone was eyeing the house. I didn't see anyone, but my gut told me that something was wrong.

My heart pounded as I raced through drawers, cabinets, closets, and pockets in search of money. I looked for things of value that I could carry with me. They had a nice TV, and lot of videos, but I could not find any cash.

I then rushed down to their basement, and continued searching. But while I was in the basement, I heard police sirens that sounded like they were about a minute away. "Someone saw me, and called the cops!" I panicked.

I sprinted back upstairs and peeked through the curtains again, and saw cops coming coming around the corner, with their sirens turned off. Two cars stopped in the front of the house.

I crawled through the dog exit, ran through the back yard, and dove over a fence into a neighboring yard. Police cars sped down the streets throughout the neighborhood, looking for me. I snuck between houses, and slowly made my way to a busy intersection, where a cop car sped right past me. I made it to safety. I entered a yard, and sat behind the trunk of a big oak tree that was in that yard, and I stayed there for hours.

Finally, when I saw kids walking by the yard, I figured the school day had ended. So I came out from behind that tree, and made my way home.

While most eleven-year-olds were studying books, I was studying people and their habits and their homes. I spent more time than I should have doing things like that.

While I was getting an education in the streets that would help me later in life, it was only a matter of time before I suffered the consequences of missing so much school.

22

We moved to 1700 Billings Street, in Aurora, Colorado. It was there that I started stealing cars. One night, when I was about eleven years old, mom and Doyle went out to the club, and left me alone to babysit Noah. After Noah went to sleep, I decided to walk to the store, which was a few blocks away, to get something to drink. On my way to the store, I saw a car parked on the street. It was still running and had its lights on. I looked to see that the doors were unlocked, and the keys were still in the ignition. I also did a quick scan of the area to see who the car might belong to, but no one was around. That car was begging me to steal it, but previous experiences had taught me that I was too short to see over the steering wheel without pillows to prop me up.

My adrenaline started rushing again, and I shot back to my apartment on foot, grabbed two pillows, then hurried back toward the car. The car was still there. I opened the door, threw my pillows on the seat, jumped in, put it in drive, and hit the gas. The engine hollered but the car didn't move. My heart almost stopped because I knew the car's owner would be appearing at any moment.

I looked to see what was wrong. The emergency brake was on. I released it, and peeled off. I drove down back streets, and got out of that neighborhood.

At eleven years old, I drove down Colfax Avenue, a major street, for about thirty minutes from Aurora to downtown Denver, and did some sight-seeing. I looked at the golden dome of the State Capital building by night. It was gorgeous!

Then I drove by Vaughn Elementary where I attended third and part of fourth grade, until mom moved us to Long Beach with Doyle. I actually got out and walked around the playground for a while. Then I drove by Lynn Knoll Elementary, where I went to school for the last part of fourth, and all of fifth grade. I then drove to South Middle School, where I attended sixth grade. Finally, I drove by East Middle School, where I was enrolled for seventh grade. I drove all over Denver and Aurora having a blast.

But I needed to get home to make sure Noah, my baby brother, was okay. So I made a right onto Colfax, got into the middle lane started heading home, when I got stopped by a red light. I looked in the rear-view mirror and I saw a cop car in the distance. I almost ruined a perfectly good pair of underwear!

The cop was about a block behind me, or about football field away, and he was driving in my direction!

"No! No! No!" I was about 80 yards away from getting caught! There were no other cars on the street. It was just me and that cop. I couldn't run the red light because he would have easily seen me and busted me. I couldn't turn right from the middle lane, because number one, it was against the law, and number two, I would have looked suspicious, turning from a middle lane.

"Please, turn green, please turn green. Light please turn green," I begged as my palms began to sweat. The cop car was getting closer and closer, and the light was still red. He was still behind me in the middle lane, so maybe he won't notice me, I hoped.

When he was about fifty yards away from the stoplight, the cop got over into the left lane, which would have put him right next to me at the red light. If he stopped

Manny Scott

at the red light, he was going to look over to his right, and see me.

"No, no, no. Light please turn now. Please, please please!" There was no way I could have gotten away from that cop car, and I knew it. My turns were mediocre at best.

My sphincter and every other muscle in my body tightened, "If I get arrested, Noah will be at home alone. What will happen to him if I get caught? Mom and Doyle are not there. I am not there."

"I can't get caught! I can't go to jail." I was about to start crying out of fear, panic, anxiety. The pressure was unbearable. I could hear my heart beating in my throat, and my whole body starting trembling uncontrollably.

When the cop was about ten yards behind me, I unlocked my door, so I could get ready to run for my life. My hand was on the door handle, shaking.

Just then, the light turned green, and and the cop accelerated right past me. I didn't move. Instead, I just sat there trembling in relief.

I took my foot off the brake, and the car slowly accelerated. I turned off Colfax street the first chance I got, and I pulled into an old apartment building where several of the lights were dim or barely flickering. I pulled up next to the building, turned off the headlights, and I put the car in park. I turned off the car, and I sat there for about 5 minutes to catch my breath and to calm myself down.

I looked around to see if anyone was looking, and when the coast was clear, I got out of the car, and jogged home. As I got back to my street, cop cars were parked near the spot from where I had originally taken the car. I went around the block, entered my apartment complex from another direction. When I made it to my building, I ran up the stairs, through my front door, and closed it. I rushed to check on Noah. When I cracked the bedroom door, I saw my little guy still sound asleep, the way I had left him.

Relieved, I walked into the bathroom, looked in the mirror, at my face and eyes and hands. I was still shaking. I went back into the bedroom with Noah, peeked out the window at the cops to see if they were on to me, and I thought about how close I had just been to being taken to jail for stealing a car. I laid down on my bed, and my head fell straight onto my mattress. I had forgotten to take my two pillows out of the stolen car. Oh well! I figured it was much better sleeping in my own bed without pillows than sleeping in jail with them.

23

I was asleep in the couch, when I felt it being lifted off the ground. Then it got slammed down. Startled, I sat up to see what was going on, and mom was standing there. She looked really angry. The front door was still open. A few moments later, Doyle walked in. Mom screamed some expletives.

"Oh no! Here we go again," I thought. The muscles in my body began to tense up.

Mom said something about some man she hit in the head with a huge beer mug. "He kept asking me to dance, and I kept telling him no," mom explained to Doyle.

"Then why did he keep coming onto you if you weren't sending him signals?" Doyle asked.

"I told him to leave me alone, and he kept pestering me! What did you want me to do? And why didn't you do something? Were you scared of him, Doyle? You're a big freakin' punk! You didn't do anything so I broke that beer mug on his head. Forget him, and forget you!" she said as she stormed off to the bedroom and slammed the door.

Doyle followed her to the bedroom, and he slammed the door too. They continued arguing in the room, when I heard a slap. He had hit momma again. I heard a fight ensue, and I heard my mom saying, "get off me!" He hit her again, and I could hear her hit him back.

She started screaming, "Lito! Call the police! Call the police!"

I got on the phone and called the cops. As soon as I hung up the big old, dial-up, rotary phone, I looked up and saw Doyle standing there. He snatched the phone from me, and I backed away from him. He threw the phone at me, hitting me in the chest with it.

"Leave my momma alone!" I said.

"Shut your freakin' mouth," he replied.

"No! You shut yours, and leave my momma alone!"

He could see courage in my eyes, "when you think you bad enough, boy, you just let me know." He went outside for something, and before he could come back in, my mom ran out of the bedroom and slammed the door, and locked him out.

She put the chain on the door too, providing extra security. He tried to get back in, and cussed her out. "Open this door! Open this freakin' door, Rose! I'm not messin' around with you, woman! Open the freakin' door or I am going to kick your behind!"

She told him, "go away and sober up!"

He had his house keys on him. He unlocked the door but the chain stopped him. He tried to break the chain with his hand. Unable to get through, he then tried to squeeze his arm through the door to grab my mom.

"Go away, Doyle! Get out of here!" She hollered.

"I'm gonna mess you up!" He fumed.

She went to the kitchen and grabbed a butcher knife, "leave us alone, Doyle. I'm tired of this!"

He persisted, trying to break the door down. Seeing that the gold chain was about to break, mom rushed the door to try to hold it closed, but Doyle was able to grab her.

Mom stabbed Doyle's hand with the knife, and he yelped. "You stabbed me! You done messed up now!"

The cops pulled up, and Doyle backed away from the door. The cops came to the door, and ordered momma to open it. The cops had their guns drawn when they entered. They told us to get on the floor. They put handcuffs on momma.

I pleaded with the cop, "My mom was just trying to defend herself. He hit her first…please don't take my momma to jail."

Momma hollered instructions at me while they escorted her to the police car, "Lito, go get Noah, and call your aunt Molly or your Aunt Gloria, tell them to come and get you." They pushed mom's head down into the car, closed the door on her, and I began crying.

"What am I gonna do now?" I wondered. My mom was in jail, and I was eleven years old.

The cop car drove off with mom in it, and I just watched the back of her head as they turned onto the street and drove off. I had tears in my eyes. Doyle was upstairs, standing outside the apartment door.

He said to me, "Lito, come in the house."

"My mom's going to jail because of you!" I ran off into the night. I walked several miles to the home of one of my friends, and stayed the night there.

24

About a month after mom got out of jail, I was sitting on the couch watching T.V. when she broke some pretty disturbing news to me, "Lito, me and Doyle are gonna get married."

I didn't say a word. I just looked confused. Doyle had done so many things to hurt us, and even after they got back together, they fought constantly, and yet they were now going to be getting married? I was only about twelve years old by then, but it didn't take an adult to know that their relationship was not the healthiest.

Then she stuck the knife in even deeper, "And, we're moving to Long Beach after the wedding."

That was it! "Oh no I'm not! I am not going back to Long Beach with him."

"You have to come with me. It's gonna be better this time around, mijo," she assured.

I wasn't convinced. "If you want to be stupid enough to marry him, and go back to California with him, you can go. But I'm not goin'…I want to live with my brothers."

"I don't want to go without you." She tried to do the guilt trip thing.

"Well then don't go, because I'm not going."

After going back and forth for a minute, she put her foot down. "You have to go. You're not staying here. You can't stay with your brothers. You have to come with me."

I was on the verge of tears because I knew she had made up her mind. "But momma, I don't wanna go back to

Long Beach. I want to stay with my brothers. I like it with them better anyway. I don't want to live with Doyle."

She tried one last appeal to change my mind. "I'll buy you a scooter if you go to California with me."

That was enough to change my mind. I was barely twelve years old, and what twelve year old boy would not like to have a scooter? As naive as I was, the thought of owning my own scooter outweighed most of the disdain I had for Doyle.

A few months later, mom and Doyle got married at the Red Rock Amphitheater, in the Rocky Mountains of Colorado, and they began making arrangements for us to move to Long Beach. They rented U-hauls, scoured the area for boxes, and packed all our belongings.

I'll never forget the pain of having to say goodbye to Juan and Jose. A couple days before we departed for Cali, mom drove me to Sterling to say goodbye to my brothers and grandma.

I got there, and we went for a walk while mom and Grandma talked. We walked to the school down at the end of the street and shot the basketball around.

We played HORSE and talk about upbeat things during the game, pretty much joking around, avoiding the inevitable.

"So, you're going to California, bud. Dang, well make sure you get a lot of girls, bud."

I laughed, trying to be strong.

They continued, "Just don't get any pregnant."

"I don't really wanna go, but mom promised me a scooter," I explained

They were like, "no way! She never offered to get us no scooter! I'm jealous, bud," they joked.

"I was going to run away so I could stay with you guys, but I really want that scooter." I continued, "Once she gives it to me, I'm gonna ride it back to Colorado and be with you guys." We all laughed, but beneath the laughter was a lot of pain and sadness.

Juan got serious. "If Doyle tries to put his hands on mom or you, you kick his butt bud. Or, you call us, and we'll come out there and kick it for you."

Mom drove up to the court, "Guys we gotta get ready to go." We all got in the car, but nobody was talking because we knew that the end was near. I looked out the window, trying not to lose it in the car on the way back to grandma's, but I was sitting in the back seat between my brothers. Jose had his left hand on my right knee, and he just kept patting it. He wasn't saying anything either. Juan had his hand over my shoulder, and kept rubbing my head. He said, "I'm gonna miss you, bud. You be strong out there, okay." Without looking at either one of them, all I was able to get out was a little, "um huh."

We pulled up to grandma's, and we all got out of the car. Grandma came out, and mom gave her a big hug.

"Come here, mi hijo!" Grandma began crying. "Grandma loves you. Te amo mucho, Lito mio, (which means, I love you a lot, my Lito). Gramma's going to miss you so much. You be a good boy out there...Come home and visit grandma, okay, mijo."

Smothering my face in gram's shoulder, I mumbled that I would visit her.

Mom tried to comfort everyone, "I'm gonna send Lito back next summer to spend time with you guys."

"I'll get to stay the whole summer, momma?" I asked.

"If your grandma and brothers say it's okay." So I looked at them, and they affirmed, "of course, bud."

I started crying. My brothers engulfed me, both hugging me, in a group hug. Their heads were together, and they were rubbing my head. We were all crying, sniffling, not wanting it to end. I didn't want to leave my brothers. I didn't really care about the scooter. I wanted my brothers. I didn't understand it then, but in that moment of saying goodbye to them, it hit me that I was losing my covering. My brothers protected me. They made sure me and mom were okay. Now, in Long Beach, it's just gonna be me.

I climbed into the back seat of the car. The sadness turned to resentment. I didn't want to look at mom. I wanted to be alone. I could not understand how could she take me so far away from my brothers. I kept asking mom, "Why can't we all be together? Why can't Juan and Jose come with us, momma? Why?"

My brothers were standing next to my door. They had their hands over one another's shoulders, and they were crying. Mom backed up the car, and I was trying to be strong. I wiped my tears away, and said, "I'll call you guys," I said. "I'll be back. I love you guys."

Tears were falling from their eyes too. "Love you too, bud."

It was one of the most heartbreaking things in the world to have to leave my brothers in Colorado.

We drove off, and I looked through the back window at my brothers, and I kept waving goodbye to them. They were waving back. Just like I looked out the back window at our house when I was five years old, when mom abruptly moved us from Sterling to Denver, I stared through the back window again. Only that second time, I wasn't staring at a house; I was saying goodbye to my brothers.

I laid down on my stomach, with my face in my arm, and I cried for over an hour.

I tried one last time to convince my mom to bring my brothers with us. "Mom, why can't they come with us? Why? Momma, please."

"Maybe later, Lito," she said. "We're gonna be okay, and you're gonna get a scooter. It's gonna be fun."

25

When we moved to Long Beach, I started eighth grade at Jefferson Middle School, and I did relatively well for a while. I even won an award for being the most dedicated musician, or trumpet player, or something like that. Of all the things I did in eighth grade, learning to play the trumpet was one of the most fulfilling. I used to spend hours practicing the trumpet. In a strange way, the music I played spoke to my soul in powerful ways. Of course, at the time, I didn't understand it in that way. But as I look back, I now see that music had a positive impact on me.

But everything else I hated about school seemed to return. Somewhere between eighth grade and enrolling at Woodrow Wilson High School for ninth grade, I started falling back into some of my old ways. My old habits, beliefs, values, and self-sabotaging ways were reemerging; and, though momma and Doyle didn't fight much initially, their old ways returned as well. It didn't take long to see that the only thing that really changed about us was our location.

One night after going out to a club, mom ran into the house, and said, "Lito, Doyle's mad. Get ready."

That could only mean on thing in my mind- it was going to be another long night. So I put on my shoes, and told mom, "momma, let's go! Let's get outta here! I don't want to do this tonight."

"No, Lito, he's coming. He's gonna hit me, Lito."

I opened the door to leave, "Momma, I'm not doing this. Let's get outta here. Let's go before he comes."

"No, don't leave, Lito. Don't leave me here alone with him. He's gonna hit me."

"Momma, this is stupid! You can stay if you want to, but I am out! I'm tired of this! Let's go! Let's go! Let's go!" I started walking out the door.

But mom pleaded with me, "Lito, please don't leave. Don't leave. He's gonna hurt me. Don't leave."

I was scared and angry at the same time. I could have gotten away and avoided Doyle, but I didn't want to leave momma. However, if I stayed, I was probably going to have to fight him, which I did not want to do either. Do I leave and let mom get hurt, or do I stay and risk getting hurt myself?

I closed the door, locked it, and sat down on the couch, and waited for Doyle to arrive.

Sure enough, a few minutes later, he unlocked the door with his key, stormed in.

I tried to slow him down, "Doyle, leave my momma alone."

He ignored me, and went into the bedroom with my momma, and started threatening her. Things escalated, and I heard mom saying, "No! Stop! Get off me! Stop it!"

He was trying to rape my mom.

I just couldn't take it anymore. Rage soon replaced my fear, and I hollered through the door, "Bitch, you better leave my momma alone or I'ma fuck you up! You always told me that when I thought I was bad enough to take you to let you know. Well, nigga, I'm ready!"

The door opened, and he looked at me. He rushed toward me, and tried to grab me, but I quickly moved out of his way, causing him to miss.

I thought about all the times he hurt my momma, and the time he hurt my brother, and the time he put us out on the street even though momma was pregnant, and I decided in that moment that I would rather die fighting than live in fear of Doyle.

I squared up with him. He came toward me, and I, with all my might and pent up rage side-kicked him in the chest. He flew backwards and hit his head on the edge of a coffee table. He was unconscious.

That was the last time he put his hands on my mom.

After that fight with Doyle, I started ditching school again. Things got so bad that I ditched school three to four days a week the first semester of my freshman year in high school. I ditched school so much that I no longer knew anyone in my classes, and I no longer felt comfortable going to class. I felt so out of place because I was so far behind on all my homework assignments. Mentally, emotionally, socially, I was so far behind that it was much easier to ditch than it was to go to school. I had been managing to write my own re-admission slips, excusing my absences, and I had mastered how to forward all of phone calls we received from the school (I used to forward all calls to the pay-phone on the corner of our block).

During Christmas break from school, mom and Doyle were at work, and I went outside to check the mailbox to make sure the school had not sent anything to my house. I opened the mailbox, flipped through the mail, and I saw something from my school. Since it was from the school on Christmas break, I figured it had to be my report card for the fall semester.

I opened it and saw that I had earned a 0.6. G.P.A. for the semester. I had 3Fs, 3Ds and a C. As bad as they were, I honestly wasn't phased one bit by them. I guess I kind of expected them to be unremarkable. I crumbled my report card, stuffed it in my pocket, and went back into the house.

The crazy thing is, despite how despondent I had been in school, I still played trumpet in the Long Beach Junior Concert Band. It was a city-wide marching band led by a man named Marvin Marker.

While I missed school three or four days a week, I almost never missed band practice, because I think it was one place where I felt safe. I didn't have to act hard. I didn't have to watch my back. In a strange way, I felt like I belonged.

It was in the trumpet section that I sat next to a guy named Alex Giraldo. Alex was a junior at Long Beach Polytechnic High School, my high school's rival. Alex was very smart. We used to spend a lot of time at rehearsal talking about girls, about family, about music, and about life. He was a very down-to-earth guy who got along with most people. He had a great sense of humor, and loved to play with people.

Like me, Alex had another side to him. He liked to steal. He taught me some really effective ways to break into cars and steal things. We spent many days and nights doing things like that. It didn't take long for Alex to become my best friend.

I couldn't wait for band rehearsal so I could see my boy. We had rehearsal once a week, on thursday nights, and sometimes on tuesdays nights for special rehearsals. Even though I missed school a lot, I never missed rehearsal. I played in the Hollywood New Years Eve Parade, next to Alex. We joked together, and had a great time clowning around.

Alex let me borrow his shoes and clothes on more than one occasion. I guess he saw that some of my shoes had holes in them, and that some of my clothes were not the best. He was very generous, even giving me the shirt off his own back. He was that kind of guy.

Well one night, February 1st, 1992 to be exact, Alex called me and told me that he needed to stop by to pick up some shoes and a shirt that he had let me borrow. I waited up for Alex until about two or three in the morning, but he never showed up. Because it was the early 1990s, cell phones and beepers weren't yet available. So I couldn't just call Alex to see if he was still coming over. But Alex almost always did what he said he was going to do, I figured something came up, or that maybe he had gotten sick, or something.

When I looked for Alex the next day, I discovered something much worse had happened to him.

26

The next day, when I went to band rehearsal, I had a bag of Alex's things, hoping to return them to him, but discovered that Alex had been killed. I stopped breathing. I couldn't hear anyone talking.

I later found out that some guys who had been bullying Alex devised a plan to set Alex up, and kill him. The police report said that two of the guys tricked Alex into believing that he could trust them, that things between them were cool. Those two guys then convinced Alex to hang out with them. They picked him up in a car, and drove Alex to a park in San Pedro, California, where two more guys were waiting. One of them jumped out from behind some bushes and punched Alex in the face, and then two of the others began punching Alex too. Alex was trying to defend himself but they were too strong. Alex fell to his knees, and one of the guys, named Michael McDonald, standing behind Alex, started strangling Alex with guitar wire that he had garroted with two washers.

Then, while Alex was struggling to break free from the wire that those cowards had around his neck, he fell face down on the ground. Michael, the guy strangling Alex with the guitar wire, switched off with one of the other guys, who continued strangling him. Alex's body went limp while he was fighting for his life, face down on the ground. Thinking he was dead, the four guys picked him up, carried him to the edge of the bluff in the park, and they threw him off. His body slid down the cliff about 15 or 20 feet.

Police reports said that Alex was still alive on the side of that cliff, but the ringleader went back down the side of the cliff to make sure Alex was dead. When he saw that Alex was still alive, fighting to breathe, he took out a knife with a wooden blade and stabbed Alex in his throat, effectually ending my best friend's life. The knife went so deep that the coroner found chunks of wood from the knife's handle in Alex's neck.

The next morning a jogger was running on the beach and saw Alex's lifeless body dangling on the side of that cliff, and called the cops.

I'll never forget the night I walked into the funeral home to say goodbye to my best friend. In the front, center of the room I can still see his brown casket. It was open. I froze at the back of the room, and just stared at it. I did not want to see my friend like that, but I felt I had to say goodbye. I took very slow, small steps until I was standing next to his casket, by myself.

There he was. The guy who was so full of life was now lying there lifeless. I looked at his eyes, and they were closed. His lips were closed too, but they just didn't look right. I looked at his neck, and even though the mortician did a good job of putting makeup over the wounds, I could still see on Alex's neck some of the wire marks from the guitar wire.

His hands were crossed, and I saw wire marks on the outer corner of his palms, letting me know that Alex fought with all his might for his life. I looked down to my right, and I saw his baby sister curled up like a ball near his casket. His mother was sobbing in the background.

That was the saddest day of my life.

I pulled an envelope out of my pocket, and laid it on his chest. In it was a letter I wrote to Alex, saying things I never got to say to him. I spent two full days writing the letter. I wrote through the tears and tremendous heartbreak, trying to tell Alex things I never got to say. I thanked him for being so kind to me. I thanked him for being my friend. I thanked him for helping me to laugh when I felt like crying. I thanked him for never making fun of my shoes or clothes. I thanked him for letting me wear his clothes so I wouldn't be so self-conscious about mine. I thanked him for accepting me, for loving me, and for being my friend-one of the only true friends I had ever really had. I put my heart in the letter, sealed it in an envelope, and I laid it on his chest, hoping that he would somehow be able to read it; and, hoping that it would somehow make me feel better for having gotten it out. While writing that letter helped me to focus on all of the things I was thankful for, I could not shake the tremendous sense of loss that still held me in its merciless, unrelenting grip.

While standing over my friend's fallen frame, I tried to say something to him, but I couldn't. Words would not come out. They were stuck in my throat. Finally, I placed my right hand on Alex's cold, lifeless hand, and I just stood there, numb. When Alex died, something inside me died too…

27

On April 29, 1992, some guys and I were glued to the television. We were waiting for a jury to convict the cops who had brutally beaten Rodney King. About one year prior, on March 3, 1991, a black man, Rodney King, was driving with two friends in Los Angeles, California. The police attempted to pull them over, but he did not stop. A high-speed chase ensued, sometimes going as fast as 115 miles per hour over freeways and through neighborhoods. Finally, when Rodney King stopped the car, he was brutally beaten. Rather than following their usual procedures, which was to tackle and then handcuff a suspect, the police officers tasered King, and kicked him in the head, and beat him with batons for over one minute. Videotape taken by a bystander showed that King was on the ground crawling, and no officer tried to tackle or cuff him. Instead, they beat him mercilessly for over one minute and nineteen seconds.

The nation had been waiting for justice to be served. Surely, those cops would be penalized for abusing their power, I thought. Surely they would be convicted. The videotape clearly showed an unarmed man being beaten by police who obviously had no regard for justice. Black and brown people everywhere who had been mistreated and abused by crooked cops believed that those crooked cops would finally pay.

I had met so many cops like that through the years-racist, condescending, overcompensating terrorist with a badge- who mistreated black and brown youth in so many ways. They would spit at us while they drove by. They threw us on the hoods of police cars and called us "worthless niggers."

I reasoned, "Finally, someone caught those monsters on tape for what they have been doing to us. It's about time!"

I hoped they would go to jail, for all the people they screwed, who are now locked up. I wanted them to pay for all those beatings they unjustly handed out while hiding behind those badges.

So I, and many others, hoped they got served for all the vitriol and hatred and mistreatment they had so gratuitously handed out to me, my family and my black and brown friends.

Then the jury read the verdict: NOT GUILTY!

I remember the outrage. We couldn't believe it.

Those cops were clearly guilty, and they still got off. That verdict made it clear to me and so many of us who lived in our neighborhoods, that black, and sometimes brown, people were on our own when it came to matters of justice in America. Clearly black victims didn't have the same value, or get the same justice, as white victims. It felt as though we had no rights that white people were bound to respect. We felt that when we most needed the law to protect us, it entirely deserted us. That verdict confirmed for me that in America, there are two kinds of people in the eyes of the law: black people and victims. In America, if an unarmed black man is getting beaten by cops, or is shot, then he must have done something wrong, simply because he is black. It became infuriating that I was incapable of being seen as a victim in the eyes of our criminal justice system. That verdict pretty much told us that we weren't worth crap.

At the time of the Rodney King verdict, I didn't know that almost one in four black men between the ages of 20 and 30 were under the supervision of the criminal justice system on any given day. I didn't know that for white men in the same age group, the corresponding statistic was only one in 16. I didn't know that blacks were more likely than whites to have been shot at by police, or that we were 18 times more likely to be wounded and five times more likely to be killed. I didn't know that prosecutors were more likely to pursue full prosecution, file more severe charges, and seek more stringent penalties in cases involving defendants of color, particularly where the victim was white. And I didn't know that blacks and latinos were sentenced to prison more often and received longer terms than whites convicted of similar crimes and with similar records. I sensed it, and believed it; but I didn't know it.

So, when those cops were acquitted, there was a collective indignation among us. I felt boiling in my soul an anger against the police, the government, and every elected official, because it seemed as though most of them were against us. We felt there was no hope for fairness in the world for people like us. It really was an every-man-for-himself mentality. Rodney King was essentially lynched by those police officers, and they were acquitted.

We believed that someone had to pay for the justice that we were so often denied. For years we had been the victims of racism and racial profiling. For years we had been manhandled and disrespected by police. For years they had gotten away with mistreating black and brown people, and we just would not accept one more miscarriage of justice against us.

While watching T.V., we saw people in LA looting, and we saw some guys beating up a white guy in South Central, Los Angeles. They pulled him out of a semi-truck, and beat him. One of the guys hit him in the head with a brick. They walked by and stomped his head. They were pulverizing that poor man. Part of me felt like it was wrong to hurt that man like that, because he himself hadn't done anything wrong.

However, the anger among black and brown people was not against any one white person in particular, but against injustice in general. The anger was about paying back all the white people who had ever done us wrong. It was about retaliating against all those who had mistreated us, who had taken advantage of us. It was a rage against all those who had talked down to us, and kicked us out of their stores even though we intended to buy something. Our outrage was a gutteral response to all those white people who had for years treated us like second-class citizens. Although I knew it was wrong, Reginald Denny, the white man who was being beaten in the middle of the street just happened to be at the wrong place at the wrong time, we reasoned.

I remember saying to myself, "momma was right. If white people have to pick between standing up for a black person or a brown person, and standing up for one of their own, most of them will always pick their own."

We had had enough. So we jumped in the car, and rode downtown, to the corner of a shopping mall where a large crowd of livid protesters had accumulated. As we pulled up, I could feel their fury. It mirrored my own. I was not alone in my outrage. My friends and I jumped out of the car and joined the multitude. Like a powder keg, we were all itching to explode. We had had enough.

Several police cars were parked in the intersections, blocking traffic from further populating the already congested area, and an army of uniformed officers were standing together, shoulder-to-shoulder, clenching their batons and shields, at each of the street corners, trying to intimidate us.

But I wasn't scared. Not anymore. I was more through than scared. Through being disrespected by them. Through being abused by them. Just through. But at fourteen years old, I lacked the lexicon to express exactly how through I was. I had no access to words that could articulate my anguish. I had no dictionary to help me describe my disgust. So, unable to verbally vent my vitriol, I picked up a brick and threw it at a police officer's car, shattering his window. That brick was my manifesto. It was all I could say at the time.

It has been said that the most dangerous person in the world is the one who feels as though he has nothing to lose. If that is true, then I, as a teenager, was very dangerous. I had already lost so much- my family was in disarray; my best friend had just been brutally murdered; and, my hope that things could ever get better for me had been thoroughly extinguished.

You see, as a young man, I was convinced that I would not live to see my eighteenth birthday. I believed that my end was near. I believed that my story was over. So, after I busted that cop's window, and he started coming toward me, my entire being concerned itself with one unconscious, yet fundamental question: "What more do I have to lose?"

Undaunted, then, I picked up a beer bottle, looked directly at him, and, with all my might, I chucked it at him. The bottle missed him, and shattered on the street. When the crowd saw my defiance of the cops, who, in our eyes, represented a broken and corrupt criminal justice system, it erupted in ways that could have gotten me killed.

People started throwing rocks and bottles through the mall's windows. They began pushing against the police shields. The stronger guys in the group lifted up the metal cage that was protecting the stores, bent the bars with their sheer strength, and broke the windows with their feet, bricks, and whatever else they could throw.

My boys and I made plans to meet up later at my house. "Don't get shot, and don't get caught," someone said before we scattered to get away from the cops. I ran toward the mall, whose stores were now being thoroughly ravaged.

I squeezed under one of the bent cages, through the pieces of glass and saw people scurrying everywhere I looked. The electronics section of a store was being ransacked. I heard glass shattering, and saw people running through the store with stereos, speakers, televisions, radios, and all kinds of electronics.

All the expensive stuff had already been taken. So I started grabbing shirts- button up shirts, rayon shirts, silk shirts. I grabbed about twenty or thirty hats too. The things in my hands were literally stacked up to my neck. I saw the army of police coming toward the store, so I started sprinting toward the exit. But as I was running, there was a guy standing in the aisle in front of me, blocking my path to the exit. I honestly don't know what he was doing. I hollered, "Move, man! 5-0 is coming!" But he either didn't hear me, or didn't want to.

With the police now entering the store, I didn't have enough time to get around the guy. My only way out was through him. So, still sprinting, I ran towards him, and like a relentless NFL fullback, I lowered my shoulder, and blasted him into the display cases. He flew forward.

I dropped a couple things, but kept running. I squeezed through the cage and people were scampering to the left, so I dashed to the right, toward the alley. Once there, I slowed down, and began to jog through the alley with my hands still full of the items I had just grabbed from the store. People whose apartments faced the alley saw me from their balconies. They were on their cordless phones, and looked like they were calling 911.

Once I exited the alley, there was a cop car speeding towards me. They jumped out of their car, and started coming toward me. With my heart racing, I cut between buildings. We were in an all out foot race, and I refused to get caught. I ran with everything I had, but the cops were gaining on me. So I dropped all but one of the hats, and all but one or two of the shirts I had looted.

I jumped a fence, and they jumped it too. I jumped another fence, and they were still on my tail. I kept running, between buildings, and when I had a little separation between me and them, I jumped into a dumpster and closed the lid. I heard them run right by me. I stayed in that dumpster for several minutes, until I was sure they were gone. When I opened the lid, there was another person on a balcony who saw me. I took off running again. After a couple hours of playing hide-and-seek with the cops, I finally made it home.

28

I was just getting more and more reckless. Subconsciously, I think we were fed up with injustice. Another part of our misdeeds just grew out of the fact that we were lost, misguided young men.

We once broke into a building, and while we were inside, several cop cars surrounded the building. Everyone panicked and scattered like roaches. We somehow thought we could make a better escape if we made it to the roof. So we climbed up to the room hoping to get a better view of where the cops were, and a better sense of which way we should run. However, there was a police helicopter hovering above the building.

One of my friends jumped off the roof and took off running, but a cop car pulled up on him and held him at gunpoint.

Some of the other guys jumped off the roof and tried to run for it too. Everywhere I looked it seemed as though I saw cops chasing my friends. I saw another one get tackled.

I knew that if I were going to have a chance to get away, that I had to take it, because I heard more sirens coming toward us.

I jumped off the building, which was at least 20 feet high, and I sprinted toward the trees. There were trees everywhere.

I looked up and saw the helicopter hovered over the trees, trying to find me. But there were too many trees. I knew I couldn't stay there long.

I stayed under the trees as long as I could, as stealthily as I could. I took off my shirt, and my hat, and I threw them in a trash can. Then, when I saw a window of escape, I took off running. I drew from all my experience of running from the cops in Colorado. I sprinted for a few blocks, and hid in some bushes behind an apartment building in the area. Cop cars rushed by, but missed me. I hung out in those bushes for about 15 minutes until the chopper flew in another direction.

During my days of running the streets, I had many close calls like that. But none were probably as dangerous as the night when some guys and I were walking down the street. A group of guys were walking in our direction. We weren't moving out of the way, and they weren't either, so we were heading straight for each other.

As they got closer, something felt really wrong. One of the guys swung at my friend Marcello, and Marcello grabbed him and threw him into the bushes, and the fight began. The other guys started fighting.

The biggest one with them was like 250 pounds, 6'2' and huge. When I moved to help Marcello, the big guy lifted his shirt with his left hand, and put his right hand on the handle of the gun that was tucked into his pants.

I froze, but started yelling for my guys to chill out. "He's got a gun! He's got a gun! Be cool! Be cool!"

Some cars started coming in our direction and the other guys ran away. As I look back at that, and so many other nights, I realize that my friends and I could have been killed.

Things like that kept happening to me, and I sensed that I was approaching my own death. My life was in a downward spiral. I was getting chased by police, I was throwing bricks at cop cars, I was getting chased by helicopters. People were pulling guns out on me.

It was in that place of brokenness that I was walking by Drake Park in Long Beach, California. And I saw a bench, and I just sat down on it. On that bench, I began thinking about my life. I was in a very dark place, an angry place, a very broken place. I remember thinking things like, "people like me- we ain't supposed to make it! Whether you are black or brown or Asian or white, and you live in my hood, something is set up for us to fail! So why should I try? Every time I try, something happens to knock me back down! Why should I try? Alex is gone, my family is a mess, life has no meaning, I have no purpose. I am done trying!"

My soul was crying out with that poet, Paul Laurence Dunbar, who said,"

> A crust of bread and a corner to sleep in,
> a minute to smile and an hour to weep in;
> A peck of joy to a pint of trouble,
> and never a laugh, but the moans come double;
> And that is life."

My entire being was in complete agreement with the existentialist philosopher who said, "life is an endless pain with a painful end."

On that bench, I was absolutely convinced that the last paragraph of my life was being written. On that bench, the last period of my life story was about to be penned. On that bench, I was certain in my soul that my story was over...

29

While sitting on that bench in Drake Park, a complete stranger walked up to me and sat down. He asked me a question, "Hey man, what you doin' out here on a school day?"

"I don't go to school no more," I said.

He shook his head. "Man I used to have a good life. I had a nice job, a good woman; I had a family," he said as his voice got a little softer. "But I threw it all away…I got addicted to cocaine and I lost my job, I lost my house, my girl left me, and I lost my family."

Then his voice cracked, "I lost everything." He then stopped talking for a moment. I looked over at him, and saw, sadness in his eyes for everything he had lost. What comes from the heart, reaches the heart, that man's honesty, and authenticity, spoke to me. He was real, and he was speaking from a very broken place.

He continued, "A little while ago, I was homeless in San Diego, laid out behind a dumpster. I had nowhere to go, no one to call on. I was laying there, looking up at the sky."

He had my attention. "But a complete stranger walked up to me and picked me up, and said, 'we gotta get you some help, big guy.'"

The man talking to me on that park bench, his name was Martin Stevens. Martin said, "all I remember is waking up, being surrounded by people who seemed like they really cared about me. They are helping me get my life together. They are helping me get off drugs. They are helping me get on my feet. They helped me find a place to live. They helped me find a job." Then he said, "I was walking home today- and I normally don't even walk this way, but while I was walking home, by this park, I just happened to look over, and I saw you on this bench."

As I look back over my life, I can't help but wonder where I would be if Martin did not look over, and see me. How many kids in the world get passed by without ever getting noticed? How many kids sit alone in cafeterias all over the world that never get acknowledged? How many young people get passed on the streets who might be on a figurative park bench in their lives, have given up, are in need of hope, and in need of someone to care enough about them to sit with them?

Martin said, "Man I am not judging you, but you seem to be going down a path that's going to get you hurt. It's going to get you killed."

I got a little defensive. I said, "man, you don't understand what I am going through."

"I don't," he replied, "but don't get mad at me. Don't get mad at me" Then he asked me to do something. "Look at me." I reluctantly looked at Martin, and he said, "just because you live in the hood, the hood don't have to live in you."

I stared at him, not sure about where he was going with that. Then he asked, "Where is your father?"

"Man, my pops is locked up," I said.

Again he said, "Look at me," and I looked at him. "You can become the man you've never met, the father you never had."

He kept going. "Where's your mom?"

"My mom is strugglin'."

"You can have a future better than your past. You can have life and life more abundantly; and this, this ain't life."

I just looked at Martin, and thought about my life, and about all of the people in my life, and I didn't see anybody, with the exception of my mother, who inspired me. I didn't see anybody whose life I wanted. I was tired of hearing my mom cry herself to sleep at night. I was tired of watching my back. I was tired of being broke. I was really tired of being sick and tired.

Martin was right, my reality didn't deserve to be called life; it was more like death. The pain of my reality was so great, my misery was so real, my despair was so dark. It was death. I was angry. I was lost in every sense of the word, and something had to change.

Martin helped me in two very important ways. First, he shared his Christian faith with me. While he was talking, the warm, loving presence that had comforted me in my room when I was seven years old (after that woman put out a cigarette on my face), was the very same presence that met me on that park bench...

What I thought was a period that marked the end of my life's sentence was actually a comma. That conversation, that encounter, that experience on that park bench is my life's defining comma. There were many commas before it, and many commas have come after it, but there have been no commas quite as defining as that one life-changing, hope-giving comma, that marked my story on that park bench.

That day I made a decision to turn the page. It has taken years to try to understand what happened to me on that park bench, but as I look back, I now know that it was there that I began taking responsibility for my life. It was there that I stopped blaming others for my shortcomings. It was on that park bench that I stopped blaming my parents for what they did, or did not, give me. It was there, on a bench, that I stopped blaming my environment for some of the decisions I was making. It was on a bench that I stopped blaming all the teachers that did me wrong. I stopped blaming all the cops that had mistreated me.

On a park bench, I realized that I had God-given power to turn my life around. I was given power to make decisions that could alter my destiny. I was given a strength to overcome my obstacles and make something out of my life. In me was a strength to improve my life. I didn't have to wait for another human being to improve my life; I didn't have to wait for someone else to come into my life to make it interesting. No, I had the power to take ownership of my choices, ownership of my future. So, on a park bench, I turned the page.

I then got up from that park bench, and I began writing new chapters in every area of my life, and I soon realized that I had my work cut out for me.

30

Turning the page- taking responsibility for your life- can happen in an instant, but writing new chapters- taking proactive steps to improve the overall quality of your life- takes time. After my experience on that park bench, I went home, and stayed in my room for a while. I didn't talk with my family about what had happened to me, because I figured they wouldn't understand. So I just stayed in my room.

I pulled the small piece of paper out of my pocket that Martin had given me, and I just stared at. It had a phone number on it. Martin told me to call the number when I got home, and to ask for a guy named Richard.

I seriously contemplated whether I should call him, because he was a complete stranger. But I reminded myself that if Martin, a complete stranger, could help me, then maybe this stranger named Richard could too. So I picked up the phone, and called Richard. When he answered the phone, he sounded happy to hear from me. I told him that a man at the park told me to call him. Richard invited me to bible study at his house that night. I wrote the address down on a piece of paper, and told him that I would try to attend.

As the time for bible study approached, I still had reservations about going to Richard's house. Yes, he sounded kind, but, again, I did not really know what he was about. I didn't know what "bible study" was really about. Plus, I had hang ups with church folks, because I had met some people who went to church, claiming to be Christians, but who were more mean than those those of us in the streets who didn't go to church.

But as I sat there in my bedroom, I heard mom and Doyle start arguing, again. Doyle was drunk, again. They went back and forth, her accusing him of being drunk; him denying it. As usual, they began verbally attacking each other. For the first time ever, I felt sorry for them. All their fighting drained me. All that fighting had to be exhausting to them.

In any case, I didn't want to be around their fighting anymore. I didn't want to listen to them fussing anymore. I was just tired of it. I picked up the piece of paper with Richard's address on it, and said to myself, "what do I have to lose? It has to be better than being here."

I walked for about thirty minutes to Richard's home. It was a small, white house, with stairs that led up to the front porch. I walked up the stairs, and knocked on his door. Richard came to the door with a nice, welcoming smile on his face. He had a warmth in his eyes. I felt his heart. He opened the door. I extended my right hand to shake his hand; he shook my hand, and then gave me a hug.

Inside the home were about five or six people, men and women, sitting around a round, wooden table.

Richard introduced me to the group with enthusiasm, "Guys, this is Manuel." Each person stood up and gave me a hug, and warmly welcomed me. I had never felt so accepted in my life. Those people didn't know me at all, and didn't have to be nice to me, but they were.

But I was still a little uncomfortable, because it was all still new. So when Richard offered to get me something to drink, I declined. I didn't want to attract any more attention to myself. He pointed me to the open chair and told me, "we're about to get started."

Just before he started the gathering with prayer, he asked, "does anyone have any prayer requests, things that we need the Lord to help us with?"

One woman did. She asked, "Would you all please pray for me. I just lost my job, and I need the Lord to open other doors for me." The people nodded.

Another man added his concerns to the prayer docket. "Please pray for our community, that God would use us to give people hope."

The pastor's wife, Patsy, asked for prayer too. "You all, please pray for me. The doctor said that my cancer is getting worse, and that it's not looking good. I am asking God for strength for me, and for my family."

"Anyone else?" Richard asked, glancing over at me. I looked away, but then thought about my mom and family.

"Would you guys please pray for my mom and step-dad? They fight all the time," I shared. Everyone nodded, looking like they understood.

"Okay," Richard said, "let's pray."

I didn't know what to do, so I just looked at everyone else. Richard closed his eyes, and everyone else at the table closed theirs too. I then closed mine too. He began to pray, and I listened. His conversation was so personal. It sounded like he was talking directly to a person who was right there in the room with us. He began thanking God for me, "Lord, thank you for meeting Manuel at the park, on a park bench. Thank you for sending brother Martin to meet him there. Thank you for your love, oh God. Thank you for your grace and your mercy. Thank you for leading Manuel to pick up the phone and call me. Thank you for leading him to come here tonight. Lord, I pray you bless him all the days of his life. I pray that you keep him. That you watch over him. That you be with him, and give him wisdom. Lord, I pray you visit his home, and meet his mom and step-dad. Lord, minister to them, and draw them closer to you. Lord, send your peace to their home. Peace in their lives. Lord, have your way…" Richard was talking directly to God, and God was right there with us, I felt him there with me. It was that same warm presence, again.

The prayer went on like that for about ten minutes, with Richard calling out the prayer requests of the others around the table, then he ended the prayer. They then opened their bibles. I didn't have one, so someone let me borrow theirs as they read along with someone else. I don't remember what we studied that night, but I remember feeling like I was in a safe, loving, understanding place, with people who genuinely had my best interest at heart. Although that house was small, simple, and, by most standards, unimpressive, it was the most loving place I had ever been in my life.

I spent many days that summer at Richard's house, praying and studying the bible. Richard took me with him to run errands, to pass out food to people who were hungry, and to help people who were in need. He never really told me why he was doing what he was doing to help all those people; he just invited me to go along with him. By watching, and being with Richard that summer, I learned so much about unconditional love. It was so humbling to see.

Things were beginning to improve for me by the end of the summer of 1992, when mom received a letter from my school. It said, in essence, that I had dropped out, and that I was required by law to go to school.

31

My mom stormed into my room, holding the letter in her hand. "What have you been doing?" she asked. I wasn't quite sure how to answer that. I wasn't sure what she knew, and how much she knew about it.

So all I could reply with was, "what are you talking about? What's wrong?"

"This letter says that you dropped out of school! Where the hell have you been going? What have you been doing?" she asked with so much anger and confusion.

For most of my life, mom said that I was the easiest of her children to raise, because I was always very well-mannered as a child. Mom told me that when I was a baby, she and Manuel, my step-dad at the time, used to take me to the movies, and I would sit there, in my own seat, and never cry. She said I used to pay attention to the whole movie even though I was only a baby. She said I was low-maintenance, and babysitters said I was the easiest child to babysit. So, when mom found out that I had been ditching school, she was shocked to say the least.

"Momma, I'm sorry. I just stopped going. I hate school," I tried to explain, but nothing I said made any sense to her.

"I want to go back to school now, momma, but I didn't know how I was gonna tell you," I explained.

"Get dressed! We are going down to the school right now! I'll be in the car." She stormed out

When I got in the car, mom's rant continued all the way to the school. She was fuming. Disappointed. Hurt too, I guess.

We walked into the office, and the receptionist greeted us, and asked my mom the reason for our visit. My mom told the woman we were there to enroll me in school. She told us to have a seat, that someone would be with us shortly.

Several minutes went by when Mrs. Wilton walked in. Mrs. Wilton was a strong black woman who had a reputation for not taking no mess from students or parents. She was stern, and didn't really smile very often. It was obvious that she was familiar with my file, and my grades, by the look on her face. I avoided eye contact with her.

She greeted my mom and me, and told us to follow her into her office. We entered her office, and both mom and I sat down in the two seats in front of her desk. She walked around her desk, and took her seat.

She looked through my file again, remaining silent for a minute, and then looked up, at me, and began speaking. "Where have you been, young man?" she asked. I fumbled through some answer nervously.

She was not blinking. She was not smiling. She just stared, with genuine curiosity. She asked again, "How in the world could you have missed almost the entire school year?" Embarrassed, I tried to answer again, but really, my answers didn't matter. There was nothing I could say that would suffice, for her, or anyone.

She asked me, "Do you want to come back to school here?"

"Yes, ma'am. I do."

"Why should I let you back into Wilson?" she inquired, and just stared at me.

I said something like, "Miss. Wilton, I am ready to learn. I want to be here. I have changed. I'm different. I want to learn. I want to go to class. I want to do better."

Unconvinced, she said, "I am sorry, but I don't believe you. I don't think you are serious about being here. I am going to send you to Reid Alternative School."

I pleaded with her, because Reid had the worst reputation in Long Beach. People who went there were not looked upon in a positive light. Quite frankly, people there ended up as failures, in prison, or dead. While my past behavior and attitude certainly justified her in threatening to send me to Reid, I really wanted a second chance at Wilson. "Miss Wilton, I am serious this time. Please, just give me a chance. Please," I begged.

She said, "you earned a 0.6, son! You dropped out of school. You were gone way too long. Do you realize how far behind you are? Do you know how hard you will have to work just to catch up, if I let you back in?"

I honestly didn't know how far behind I was, but it didn't matter. I wanted another chance, "yes ma'am. I know I'm behind. I know I was acting a fool. I know. I really do, but please. I've changed. I'm a new person. I promise. Please, just give me one chance. Just one."

"If you mess up one time, you are out of here. You understand?" she asked, and I nodded. "You are going to have to take summer school classes. You are going to have to take zero period, and extra classes. You are going to have to get extra help. You are going to have to focus. You are going to have to work really hard," she explained. Then she looked me directly in the eyes and hit me with, "Are you really willing to do what is necessary to graduate from Wilson?"

With tears in my eyes, I said to her in the most sincere, yet humble way I could, "Miss Wilton, I am willing to do whatever it takes. I will do everything you tell me to do.

"Son, you have one chance. Don't mess it up. If you mess this up, you are out of here."

I let out a big sigh of relief. She had every right to send me to another school, but she gave me a chance. Just one, and I was determined to make the most of it.

Miss Wilton said a few final words to my mom about next steps, and then had my mom fill out some paperwork. My mom left me at the school, and Mrs. Wilton sent me over to a counselor to pick my classes. I walked over to Miss Wilton and gave her a big hug. I don't think she realized how important her giving me that second chance meant for me.

Getting re-admitted to school was one thing, but succeeding was going to a whole different beast. I was a little scared to go back to school. It's not like I had all of a sudden learned how to read better, or study more effectively. As a matter of fact, when it came to school, I still had many of the bad habits that plagued me before I dropped out. I still had unhealthy sleeping habits, staying up too late, and sleeping in. So even though I knew I was going back to school, doubts crept into my mind. "What if I can't cut it? What if I mess up? How am I going to pull this off? If I don't make it here, then I am out of here."

32

The first day of school came. I walked to school, and prayed most of the way there.

I walked through the front doors, and I found my first class, and entered. I took my seat in the back, as I always did. Because I had lived in twenty-six places before I was sixteen years old, and had bounced from school to school, I learned along the way that seats in the back of the room gave me the most freedom, and the least accountability. It was in the back of the room that I could remain under the radar, and look at my cheat-sheets, if necessary.

The first day of school was fine. The first week was fine. But the second week, the other students started to get more comfortable, and were reverting to some of the usual, bad habits that thwart learning in classrooms. People passed notes. People started clowning around, and telling jokes. They were not really taking school, or our teachers, seriously. Trying to fit in, I too started participating in some of the shenanigans. I laughed at several of the jokes, and even started telling a couple jokes of my own. Jokes about peoples' mommas. I was falling into my old, mastered habit of being present physically while being mentally absent.

But I had to break a very bad cycle, "I can't do this," I said to myself, trying to snap out of it. "I don't want to go back to doing that. I don't want to go to Reid. I don't want to waste my life," I thought. I felt it resounding in my soul, "if I keep doing what I always did, I will keep getting what I always got." That behavior had always resulted in me bad grades. It had always gotten me in trouble. That behavior never worked out well for me, because it caused me to miss many opportunities to learn.

I wanted more out of life. I wanted to do better in school. I wanted to be proud of myself. I wanted to play football. I wanted to do something with my life. I wanted to make God proud of me. I wanted God to do something with my life. The games people were playing in class weren't as funny to me as they used to be, and I had to make sure I didn't allow myself to get sucked into the silliness and mediocrity any more.

I wanted to be somebody, and to make that happen, I knew that I had to focus, even if it meant that people didn't like me. Even if it meant people would call me a square, or accuse me of trying to be white, or whatever. I wanted to learn, period.

I knew I had already missed out on so much knowledge and wisdom, and I now had a second chance to right those wrongs. I decided that I had to break some of my bad habits, and replace them with some new, more helpful ones. So when other students started telling jokes (and some of them were hilarious), I acted like I didn't hear them. I had to. When people passed notes, I tried to ignore them. I had to.

I had to make up my mind. No one else could succeed for me. No one else could live my life for me. No one else!

Aimlessness is perhaps the biggest enemy of success, and I had to focus on what I really wanted in my life. I didn't want failure, but success. I didn't want Fs and Ds; I needed As and Bs. I realized that although I could not go back and change my past, I could, from that day forward, work to create a better future, and that's what I committed to doing.

But that resolve was tested daily. For example, I was terrible at math, and I started beating myself up over it. I said things to myself like, "If you would have paid attention in class, and hadn't missed all that school, you would be further along. Now, you'll never catch up." I started feeling sorry for myself, and doubting my abilities, and at times wanted to give up. But giving up was no longer an option, and feeling sorry for yourself is one of the worst habits you can have, because it wastes time and energy. So I had to make a decision, was I going to keep trying to figure out the math on my own, or was I going to swallow my pride, and ask someone for help? "Sure, they would see how far behind I was in math, and maybe even think I'm stupid, but who cares?" I reasoned. "At least I'll learn what I need to know in order to do well on the quizzes and tests." So I often went to the library and asked for help. The tutors there didn't judge me at all. They were always willing to help and encourage me. There are a lot more good, helpful people in the world than there are bad people, I learned.

While I spent a considerable amount of time getting tutored in the library, most of the time I stayed in my bedroom, completing assignments, on my own, every night. To my delight, because I kept working at it, I started to understand math. I started getting more confident in my ability to solve basic math problems, and eventually algebra and geometry equations. After a while, I actually started really enjoying math.

I finally realized that the reason I hated math, and school in general so much, was because I never really took the time to understand it, and I didn't have a lot of people around me willing to do the work required to help me understand it. As a result, I often felt stupid, and it was a self-defeating cycle of self-pity. However, with focused study time, in a quiet place, and and with the help of others, math, and school, became fun for me.

Some guys that I used to hang out with, and waste time with, came by my house after school one day, wanting to hang out. Actually, they wanted to do something illegal. One of them had a gun, and they were planning on doing something stupid. I told them that I wasn't going with them, and I told them that they shouldn't go either. They told me to stop playing, and urged me get in the car. I tried to explain to them that I needed to finish up some things at home, and that I couldn't kick it like I used to. I told them that I had started going to church, and that I was trying to focus on on school now.

They accused me of getting soft on them. They got in the car, and left. A part of me wanted to go with them, but I knew that I had homework to do, which I knew I would not have finished had I hung out with them. I knew it.

I learned that everyone in my life was either a wing or a weight. I had people in my life weighing me down, and holding me back; and, on occasion there had been other people who had lifted me up, my wings, and they helped me grow as a person.

Sadly enough, there were even people in my family that I had to distance myself from. Not because they were bad people, but because they were not supportive of me or my mother. They were not there for us when we were down, so when things were getting better, I didn't really want to be around them. In short, I had to learn how to love some people from afar.

I decided to forgive people who were not asking for forgiveness. Frankly, I had to let go of some things people did to hurt me even though they were never sorry about the pain they had caused. I learned that I had to let go of the negativity, and the hatred, and the bitterness, and focus on the great things going on in my life. I had to focus on my future.

When I decided to improve the quality of my life, I lost a lot of people who I thought were my friends. But I decided that if nobody had my back, that nothing was going to stop me. No one was going to stop me. I had been through too much to go back. I had been too close to death to not live my life more fully, with more gratitude, and more purpose. I wanted more, and I was willing to work for more, even if I had to do it with very little support from family and people I thought were my "friends."

I made a decision to pick up my grades, I got eight to nine hours of sleep at night, I woke up early before school to prepare myself mentally, physically, and spiritually for the day ahead; I arrived at class early, I paid attention in all my classes, and I finished my homework before I watched T.V., listened to the radio, played video games, or hung out with friends; and, I made sure to ask for help whenever I needed it.

My hard work began to pay off. I got home one day and I checked the mailbox, and I saw an official looking piece of mail from the school. For the first time in years, I was not nervous. I was actually eager to see what it said. I tore open the envelope, and saw that I earned 5 As and 2 Bs my first semester back in school! I was so excited! I expected to do well, but I didn't know I would do that well.

I couldn't really believe that I was seeing those grades under my name! Teachers gave me excellent conduct grades, marking the drastic change in my attitude and demeanor in class.

Also, my attendance was nearly perfect. I'd done it! I really turned the page! That report card showed that I made the Dean's list, and that I, for the first time in my life, had made the honor roll. In one semester, I went from being a high school dropout to a distinguished student. For the first time in a long time, I stood out for something positive and fulfilling. I was proud of myself. I was inspired and more motivated than ever before to do well in school. School became fun to me, and studying became easier as time went on.

33

After picking up my grades in the fall of my sophomore year, I was cleared to join the football team for Spring training. It was always my dream to play football, but my grades were never good enough to make the team. But by my junior year, I earned a starting spot on the team as a wide receiver, punt returner, kick returner, and free safety.

I was also placed in the class of a twenty-three-year-old student-teacher named Erin Gruwell. She grew up in a gated community in an upper-middle-class family. She was on her way to law school when the Los Angeles riots broke out. She had an epiphany that she did not want to be a lawyer. She wanted to be a teacher. She said she knew she would not make a lot of money, but that didn't matter to her, because she wanted to make a difference. And she didn't just want to be any teacher, she wanted to be the kind of teacher who taught the kids that others underestimated. She wanted to teach kids that had no hope. She wanted to teach kids who felt as though they hadn't been given a chance to succeed.

So she applied to Long Beach State and began working on her teaching credential. Then she applied to teach at Wilson High as a student-teacher. Wilson at the time had 3,500 students, and she was assigned to my class. There were racial tensions on our campus, and there were gang tensions at our school. There was actually a race war on our campus. So all of those tensions spilled over, into our classroom

So when she walked into my class of African-Americans, Latinos and Asians and handful of white students, she had no idea what she was walking into. She was wearing a pearl necklace, and a white polka-dotted Julia Roberts' Pretty Woman dress. And she had in her hand an attaché case.

She then wrote her name on the board, and she turned around and greeted us, and introduced herself to us as Ms. Gruwell. She had a preppy, cheerleader enthusiasm about her that made us smile. The sentiment in the room was, "this is going to be fun!"

She passed out the syllabi with names on it like Shakespeare, Homer, Chaucer, Hemingway, Frost, and all these other people we had never heard of. She was "trained by professors who hadn't *seen* a kid in a hundred years," I heard her say later. While she was fully aware that there were many professors who had been teaching for fifty or sixty years, who were still effective, she didn't have those professors. Her professors passed down to her pedagogies and techniques that were no longer relevant in the classroom, and certainly no longer relevant for teaching kids who were crippled by poverty.

So, being ill-equipped, Miss. G. just kept showing up, and trying different things. However, regardless of her efforts, she was not effective. I'm pretty sure that it is during tough times that character is formed. When she wanted to throw in the towel, during those times when we were just getting on her last nerve, she kept showing up. When she felt like she had made a bad decision to go into education, she kept showing up. When her heart was heavy, and she felt like her work was in vain, she kept showing up. She just kept showing up, and, during that valley of testing, she humbled herself, and asked herself, "what am I

missing? What can I try differently? What can I learn from
these kids? What can I do better?" Ms. G. never gave up.
She humbled herself, and kept showing up. It was in that
context that the magic of learning began to take place in
our class.

One day, my friend, Lamar Logan, drew a picture of
Shawn Martin. Lamar was the unspoken leader in our
class. He was the alpha male of our class. So when he drew
a picture of Shawn, it circulated throughout the class.

When the drawing reached Shawn, he looked at it,
he dropped his head, and, as he put it, his "eyes started
sweating." Shawn started crying, silently, of course. Ms. G.
noticed he was unusually quiet, snatched it from him,
looked at it and turned red. And then she asked, "who did
this?" There was silence. Then she went off on us.

She started talking about intolerance and anti-
semitism and the Jewish Holocaust and how Jewish people,
because of their religion, their ethnicity, their culture, were
used as scapegoats by Hitler's regime. They were divided,
and torn apart as a people. They were forced into
concentration camps, tortured, gassed, experimented on.

Then she explained that such hatred began when
Nazis caricatured them. Jewish people were denuded of
their dignity, robbed of their personhood, and it started with
pictures like the one that made it to Shawn's desk.

When she talked about the Jewish Holocaust, most
of us had no idea what she was talking about. That became
clear when one of my friends asked her, "Miss. G. What is
the Jewish Holocaust?"

And she was taken aback, "How many of you have
ever heard of the holocaust?" Most of us did not.

She continued, "how many of you have been to
more funerals than birthday parties?" All of us had.

"How many of you have more friends in jail than in college?" All of us.

"How many of you know where to find drugs, or a gun, right now?" Again, all of us.

"How many of you are being raised by a single parent?" Most of us.

The questions became increasingly personal. The weight of our reality, the burdens we brought to school each day, finally hit her like a ton of bricks. She had this look on her face that I hadn't seen on her before.

The bell then rang, and we all filed out of class. I remember feeling that there was something different about Miss G. Most teachers never asked us about our lives, about what we lived with every day. We weren't used to teachers caring about us on that level- especially white teachers.

After that incident, she started changing her methods. She started trying new things. More importantly, she humbled herself, and started becoming a student of us. She started doing things to learn more about us.

Miss G. had an openness about her that made us feel safe and secure when we were in her presence. She had the ability to continue holding us in high regard even though she saw our issues and shortcomings. She gave us space to be ourselves, and began pushing us to grow, and to think about things differently.

She started learning a little bit about hip-hop music, about Snoop Doggy Dog, Tupac Shakur, Biggie Smalls, and many other people we, as students, looked up to. She used to try to dissect their works and teach us various things about how our heroes used language. We learned about various rhetorical tropes and figures like metaphors and similes; about voice and personification; and, chiasmus and other things that they were doing with words in their music.

She also exposed us to more than raping, rapping, rebounding and robbing, which was, and still is, what the media often showed people like us doing. She took us on a field trip to the Museum of Tolerance. I personally went on that trip expecting to hang out with my friends, and flirt with some girls, but I ended up being devastated by the tragedy of the Jewish Holocaust.

She also took me, Lamar, Shawn, and others to Pomona College. I was intimidated at first, because I believed everyone else around me was smarter than I was. However, my conversation with college students helped me see that I was smart enough to go to college too.

Ms. G took our class to see Schindler's list in Newport Beach, where I was expecting to be bored, but ended up being inspired by the heroism of Schindler.

Sadly enough, after the movie, which had a powerful message about stereotyping, bigotry and racism, I entered an elevator, about to exit the movie theater when a white woman who had also just seen the movie, clutched her purse, and turned away from me in fear. She literally faced the corner of the elevator and rushed out as soon as the doors opened.

We then went to dinner. It was during that dinner that I saw a white family- a father, mother, and a couple of children- sitting at a table near me. They seemed so happy and whole. I got a little emotional because their family seemed so in tact. The kids seemed so well-mannered, and the parents looked like they really loved each other. In my heart, I really wanted a family like that.

Once she had established rapport with us, helping us believe she really had our best interest at heart, she began doing more interesting things in class. There were days we would go into the class, and the desks would be rearranged. She would sometimes put tape on the ground and play a game with us. She was the kind of teacher who put apple cider in the back of the room and toasted for change.

Ms. G. exposed us to real Holocaust survivors and their relatives. I'll never forget the time she introduced this tall man to our class. He walked up to the lectern, and he told us about people he lost in the Holocaust. I remember him screaming, "Never again! I will never forget! I will never forget! I will never let anything like that happen again! Young people, rise up! Use your voices! Stand up against injustice!" We were all startled by his passion, but I'll never forget him. I felt his anger, and his hurt, and his love.

Ms. G. often did things that disturbed our equilibrium. She surprised us with her lesson plans. She didn't always let us know what she was about to do. She shocked us sometimes. She challenged us. She used all of her personality and resources to reach us and teach us.

She used hip-hop lyrics, poetry, R&B music, public figures- anything she thought would get our attention. She quoted Shakespeare and Snoop Dogg. She quoted Tupac and Anne Frank. She quoted Chaucer and Ceasar Chavez. She referred to Anti-sematism and Aretha Franklin. She was very creative and free. She realized that if she did not engage us at the beginning of a class period, then she would have a hard time keeping our attention for the rest of the class. So she tried all kinds of things. Some things connected with us more than others, but she just kept trying. She kept showing up. She kept speaking life into us. She kept loving us, and pushing us.

One of the things that helped me most was the way she used journals to connect with us. One day, she pulled out some journals and said, "I want you to write. I want you to tell your story. I want you to write about the time you lost your friend who was mowed down in a drive by shooting. Write about the time you had to watch your father get carried away by the cops. Write about the time you had to defend your mother. Just write. We'll deal with grammar and rules and syntax later. Right now, just start by writing from your heart."

Not all of us trusted her, but I was one of the students who did. I didn't have anything to lose, so I figured I would try.

Ms. G. knew most of us didn't know how to make our subjects or verbs agree; but she also knew that we had PhDs in urban existentialism with an emphasis in ghetto eschatology. We had a different kind of knowledge, and she did everything in her power to harness it.

"What would happen if people put down their guns and picked up a pen, and changed the world with their words?"

Ms. G provided a window into great literature for many of my classmates; for me, though, she parted the curtains, and she let the sun shine in. Ms. G helped me appreciate the beauty of the English language. She made me want to learn how to make words sing and sting, to pierce and to convey a sense of pride, and empowerment, all at the same time. So I wrote, about my pain, my dreams, my hopes, and my fears. What I appreciate most about that time is she always responded, in purple ink, to my journal entries. She encouraged me in more ways than she realized.

Then, one day, she said, "Manny, you have to go to college." No one in my family graduated from high school. She helped me see that life isn't just about where I was from, but also about where I was going, and where I wanted to go. Life is about doing what needs to be done to realize our potential. She helped me see that if I went to college, I would be able to do some of the things that I had always wanted to do. She helped me see that I wouldn't have to worry about money, and I'd be able to help my mom, and I'd be able to travel the world, and help more people who were in need.

She said, "Manny, I'll help you, but only if you let me. You have to be willing to work for it." Around that time, I was wrestling with the idea of going to the Air Force. I had always dreamed of becoming a pilot. However, Ms. G convinced me that I could go to the Air Force after I finished college, if I still wanted to.

One night, after playing basketball with her husband and his friends, we went back to her apartment, where she had a stack of college applications on her dining room table.

She asked me, "where do you want to go?"

"I don't know. What do you think?" I said.

"Why don't you to apply to my dream school, UC Berkeley. It's the Harvard, the Ivy League, of the West Coast." She continued, "I had a 4.2 G.P.A., and they didn't let me in. But you had 0.6; you were a drop out; you were a terrible student; and now you have like a 3.9. Manny, they might see your potential." She was always so enthusiastic and hopeful.

"But where is it, Ms. G.?"

"It's where Jason Kid plays basketball."

That sealed the deal for me. I said, with a smile on my face, "Yeah, that's where I want to go." The weird thing about it all is I was never really a basketball fan. I was more of a football guy. But for some reason, the way she said "Jason Kidd" was very persuasive.

I honestly didn't really think any college would accept me, but she did. She believed for me. She taught me that sometimes you have to believe in someone else's belief in you, until your own belief sets in. That's what Ms. G was for me. She was the one who believed for me. She saw my potential and kept calling me up to it. She refused to let me, or others, settle for mediocrity. She challenged us to dream bigger, and to work harder, to make more out of our lives.

I'll never forget the day I received an acceptance package from U.C. Berkeley. I honestly did not appreciate the significance of an acceptance letter from a college, let alone U.C. Berkeley.

But not everyone was happy for me. I handed my acceptance letter to Dr. Curruthers, my British Literature teacher, expecting him to congratulate me. I thought he liked me, for he had been kind to me the whole year. However, when I showed him that acceptance letter, he showed his true colors. He asked, with a condescending tone, "How did you get into U.C. Berkeley?" He didn't smile. It was not a joke. I grabbed my acceptance letter and walked away. From kindergarten to my senior year in high school, I, for some reason, had an experience like that in school. I wish more teachers realized how powerful their words are in the lives of those they teach.

A little discouraged, I then walked over to Ms. G's class. I handed her my acceptance letter and she jumped up and down, and then started crying tears of joy. She was so proud of me. "Are you gonna go? Please say, 'yes!'" She glowed. Her voice, and her enthusiasm, and her joy again persuaded me. I was thinking about going to the Air Force still, but her conviction, and the hope in her eyes, touched me on a very deep level.

"Yeah, I think so," I replied. She hugged me, and just smiled, as she kicked me out of her class so she could continue her lesson. I guess you could say I was Ms. G's first success story.

34

Not everyone was as supportive as I would have liked. When I got home, I showed my acceptance letter to mom.

"You are not going to college," she said.

"Oh, yes I am," I insisted.

"No, you're not going to college," she repeated.

"Momma, whether you like it or not, I am going to college," I assured her.

"Get out of my house!"

I grabbed some of my clothes and walked out. I couldn't believe my own mom would try to hold me back. I was devastated, and started crying. I didn't understand.

But I had made up my mind. Nothing, or no one was going to stop me from going to college. Not even my mom. I decided to get as far away from her and the disfunction as I possibly could. I was tired of fighting my mom's battles, and tired of their drama.

I drove to the beach in my Ford Escort, and slept in my car my mom and step-dad had purchased for me a year earlier.

A few days later, I went home to get more clothes, and I saw a note on my bed. It was from mom. She asked me to come home. She said she didn't want to be like her mother. I balled up her note, and threw it on the bed.

Mom then came into my room, sat on the edge of my bed, and told me a little bit about her life. She told me her mom put her out on the streets when she was younger. She told me about mistakes she's made, and I began to sense that mom was afraid to lose me. That's when it finally hit me: mom didn't really want to keep me from going to college; she was really just hurt that another woman, namely Ms. G., had had such a great influence on me. Mom was hurt because she thought I had let another woman take her place in my life. That's one of the challenges of being raised by a single-parent; they often treat their sons more like husbands.

Nonetheless, it had just been me and mom, for many years. We had been through so much together. We had been homeless together. We had fought Doyle together. I comforted her many nights. When she used to cry, I used to cheer her up. Now, with me about to go to college, mom was afraid to lose the one constant in her life.

After momma and I had our heart to heart, we hugged. Knowing that time was short, we tried to spend more quality time together.

I graduated on June 22nd, 1995 wearing my cap and gown, surrounded by a bunch of my friends. Grandma, and my brothers came all the way out from Colorado for my graduation.

I walked across the stage, received my diploma, and felt great! I felt like I had finally done something important in my family. I was the first person in my family to make it across the finish line of high school. I made it! That night, I went to grad night, and had the most amazing time. I stayed up all night.

Then, on Saturday, June 24th, 1995, I put my bags in the car, and mom drove me to the airport. By that time, my car had been stolen twice, and I could not find it after the second time.

So, on the drive to the airport, momma gave me a pep talk. It felt like kindergarten again. I joked with her to keep from crying. When we got to the airport, I checked in at the counter, and mom walked me to my gate. That was before 9/11, so people could still walk with you through security, all the way to your gate.

We sat at the gate, and talked. We kept talking to avoid the silence. There wasn't enough time. We were trying to say everything we thought we needed to say, but it was getting hard. I was excited, but sad. She went into her pocket, pulled out a $20 bill, and gave it to me.

Then the announcement was made that my flight was going to start boarding soon. I waited for others to get in line so I could spend a little more time with mom. After everyone else had boarded, mom told me to go. We both stood up, and I gave her a hug and told mom, "I love you."

"I love you too, mijo," she replied.

Then she shocked me. She said, "Have a nice life." She was holding back tears. Those words hit me hard. Momma was saying goodbye. She was letting me go, and it was hard.

I got in line, and was trying hard to keep it together. I was trying to be strong, but my heart was really heavy. I wanted to stay with my mom, but I knew I needed to go. I knew I needed to grow up.

Mom was all I ever had. Up to that point in my life, mom had been my only constant. She was the one who protected me. She was the one who nurtured me. She was the one who covered me with her jacket on the floor of that homeless shelter.

Just before I walked down the walkway to the plane, I looked back at mom one last time, and waved at her.

"I love you, Lito."

"I love you too, momma. Forever."

I boarded the plane and took my seat. It was a window seat on the left side of the plane. I looked through the window, and I saw mom standing in the window at the gate. She was crying.

I lost it. The plane pushed back until I couldn't see momma anymore.

On that plane, trying not to sob, I just started to talk to momma, even though she couldn't hear me. I remember saying, "I love you, momma. Thank you for everything. Thank you for everything." I thought about all that we went through together, and all of the sacrifices she made for us, and all of the fights, and our journey of survival. All at once, all the memories- the highs, the lows- they all flooded my mind and heart. I cried for most of the flight, thinking about my life.

That was a major turning point in my life. I had really turned the page. I was really beginning a new chapter.

But I couldn't help wondering, "Am I really smart enough for college?" After all the school I had missed, I wondered if I was I really up to par with some of the brightest students in the world? From fourth to ninth grade, I missed sixty to ninety days of school every year. Could I really compete with the best and brightest?

What I didn't know was that everything mom taught me, and all that I had learned in the streets about fighting was about to come into play in the days ahead. I had no idea what I was in for at UC Berkeley. I had no idea that I was about to be in one of the hardest fights of my life.

35

After my plane from LAX landed at Oakland International Airport, I deplaned and headed toward baggage claim. In the baggage claim area, other people were being greeted by family and friends, with hugs and laughter. I didn't have anyone there to greet me but my bags. I grabbed them, and walked out the airport doors.

While outside, I watched as people jumped into cars, taxis, onto buses, and shuttles. I walked to the shuttle that was going to take me to the BART train station. I just stood there for a moment, observing it all, "I am really alone. It's just me." All I had to my name was the $20 in my wallet, and my raggedy suitcase with holes in it. I was a little afraid. I was out there, in a strange place, on my own.

What had I done? Although I'd been somewhat independent long before that day, but the kind of aloneness I felt at that airport was different. I only had $20 to my name. I had just said goodbye to my comfort zone. To be sure, I realized that me going to college gave some people hope. I knew they were cheering for me, and I didn't want to let them down.

And, frankly, sometimes the only reason you keep moving forward is because you can't go back. Courage is not the absence of fear; courage is the decision that what you want or need is greater than what you fear. I wanted more out of life, and I now had my chance to go get it.

The shuttle arrived. I took a deep breath, I picked up my bags, said a quick prayer, and stepped onto the shuttle.

I transferred from the shuttle to the BART train, which took me to Shattuck Avenue in downtown Berkeley. I walked up Bancroft Avenue, the main street that led to campus, wearing a backpack, pulling my luggage. I walked up the street, at all the passing cars, and all the new people. I was anxious and eager all at the same time.

I walked to unit 1, to Spens-Black Hall, and checked in for the Summer Bridge program. At the registration table were a bunch of students with their parents, grandparents, aunts and uncles, and siblings. It seemed like everyone in line with me was waiting in line with an army of people. I didn't understand. I wondered, "Why are their parents here?" Dad's were carrying boxes, mom's were carrying packages, and they all seemed happy. I was an anomaly, it seemed, as I stood there alone, with no one to hold my hand.

I checked in, rode the elevator to the 6th floor, and entered my room, 608. I walked in and put my things down. I then went to the window and looked out, and saw the quad area, the dining hall, and a line of people checking in.

I unpacked my bags, and laid down on my bed, when the door opened, and in walked my new roommate- a guy who was he's 6'6", and weighed about 250 pounds. His name was Johnny Destefano, from Sacramento, California. He was on the football team too.

I left my room, and walked around the campus, to see what it was like. I walked to Telegraph Avenue, and I took in all the street venders, selling weed paraphenalia, anti-war paraphanalia, tye-dyed shirts, incense, self-made jewelry and trinkets. There were restaurants lining the streets. There was a pizza spot, Fat Slice, where the slices of pizza were huge! Down the street was Blondie's, another pizza spot with gargantuan, sumptuous pizza slices.

I walked to campus and saw Sather Gate. I walked through Sproul plaza, where I saw Rick Starr, a 50-something year old guy wearing a top hat and belting out old Frank Sinatra songs. His microphone was plugged into a coffee can. As I walked by, he stared into my eyes with a huge smile on his dirt-stained face, and sang Sinatra's "My Way," loudly, in full voice.

I walked through Sather Gate, passed Dwinelle Hall, Wheeler Hall, walked by Moffatt Library, around to Evans and LaConte, and took a break by the Campanile. Then I walked up toward Foothill street, and saw Memorial stadium.

Berkeley's campus was breathtaking. As I walked, I admired all the stately, majestic buildings. They seemed so important, so regal. So intimidating. So inspiring. I felt a sense of pride for being there. "I'm a student here. I belong here. This is my school. My campus!" It felt really good.

After my walk, I went back to my dorm for the evening's meet and greet. People from all over the country were there. The program coordinators welcomed us to Summer Bridge '95, and informed us about everything we needed to know about the the program: where to find things, where to eat, when the dining hall is open, rules and guidelines, and all that good stuff.

Then we broke up into groups based on the floor we lived on, and did a getting-to-know-you ice-breaker. On my floor was Shareef Abdur Raheem, the NBA star, Kenyon Jones, a 7'1" basketball player, Joe Cook, Johnny Destefano, who went on to have a successful career in the NFL, a guy named Robert Zaki, who had a chip on his shoulder because his parents were supposedly some bigshot lawyers and doctors.

That summer, I made a lot of friends. I used to open my dorm room window, and sing "I Got Five On It!" I used to hollar Jodeci's reknown "ooohhh Yeahhh!" It was an exciting time in my life. I got to know some really great people with whom I am still friends.

That summer, I also entered a talent show competition with my friend, Sharine Buchanan, who has one of the most amazing voices I've ever heard. In my group was also a friend named Michelle Skinner who is now a successful attorney in Florida. We won the summer's talent show by singing "I'm Available to you."

In Bridge 95, we had floor wars, where we played pranks on other people. It was really beginning to be an exciting summer, until one incident almost got me kicked out of school.

36

Summer Bridge was going great, until I was attacked by my neighbor. One morning, Johnny and I were getting ready for class, and Johnny turned on his radio. I was sitting on the edge of my bed, reviewing my math homework. Then we heard a loud sound on the wall next to Johnny's bed as though someone had hit the wall. The wall shook a little bit. Johnny and I looked at each other, a little confused because we didn't know what that was. We shrugged our shoulders, and kept getting ready for class.

A couple minutes went by when our door flew open. It was Robert, our neighbor. Robert had developed a reputation in Summer Bridge as being an arrogant white guy from Los Angeles. He often boasted that his father was a big shot lawyer, and that his mother was a doctor. Whenever he talked to you, or looked at you, it was always with an air of superiority. He often acted like he was better than everyone else. While I never personally had a problem with him, I heard several people say that Robert had rubbed them the wrong way.

Well that morning he stormed into our room, he looked pissed off. He stormed in, and looked at me, and said, "Manny, you better turn that music down, right now!" Then he turned around, and walked out. I smiled in disbelief, and looked at Johnny, who was smiling too. I couldn't believe it. "Did that just happen?" Johnny had a look on his face that said, "What in the world just happened? Oh heck no!"

Johnny then turned the music up. About a minute went by, and our door flew open again. Robert entered again. Not once did he look at Johnny. He looked directly at me, with a creased brow, and more intensity than before. He threatened, "Manny, I told you to turn that music down. You have one more chance to turn that music down, or I am going to have to resort to other means."

I thought to myself, "It's not even my radio! I didn't turn it on. I didn't turn it up! And yet, this guy comes in here threatening me? The nerve! I haven't done anything wrong!"

Even though Robert was worked up emotionally, I remained completely calm. I was not mad. I did not want to fight. But, I let my pride get the best of me, and I called his bluff. I got up, and walked toward my door, and said, "Well, go ahead, and resort to your other means then."

I stuck my head out the door, and saw Robert running toward me with his right fist cocked back.

Without much time to react, I quickly stepped out into the hallway and squared up with him. He swung at me with his right hand. I leaned back, dodging his punch. He missed. I was still completely calm. I still was not in the fighting mood. I was not mad at all. He swung at me again, and missed. To defend myself, I quickly threw a left jab, and hit him in the nose and mouth. He dropped to the ground, and squirmed in pain.

"Oh snap!!" Screamed Johnny. He stood over Robert, and screamed, "SpaaaaaccccceeeeeeeGhooooooostttt!!!"

Robert laid in my doorway, and his nose was bleeding onto the carpet in our room. I leaned over, and told him calmly, "You shouldn't have swung at me, and you better learn how to talk to me with some respect. Now get out of my doorway."

I stepped over him, went into my room and grabbed my backpack. Robert was still laying in my door way. I stepped over him again, and knocked on Kimani's, my R.A.'s, door. His room was literally across the hallway from my room. He opened the door, and I told him, "Please get this guy out of my doorway. He swung at me, and I defended myself."

Kimani looked at me, and Robert, and back at me, with total surprise. "Wait, what happened?" He asked.

I explained what happened to him again, and I told him we needed to get to class.

Johnny and I walked down the hall, toward the elevator. Robert got up off the ground, and he followed us, and started talking trash. "We're not in the jungle anymore." Johnny and I just ignored him and kept walking. He continued, "Why don't you go back to Long Beach with all the other monkeys?" Johnny and I ignored him, but that pissed him off even more. He threatened me again, yelling, "My dad is a lawyer; my mom is a doctor. You are going to get thrown out of here. Jungle people like you don't belong here. You are done! I'm going to make sure you get sent back to the jungle where you belong." We just ignored him. When the elevator door opened, Johnny and I got on. Robert kept talking while the elevator doors closed in his face. Johnny and I went to class.

After class, Johnny and I were walking back toward our room, when we ran into Devin Lonon, another friend who was on the football team. He asked "Manny, what happened? Police are looking for you." I told him that I knocked out Robert. He looked concerned, and said that the cop cars had the building surrounded.

Rather than going back to my room, which would have surely resulted in me getting arrested, I decided to go to the Golden Bear Center, now called the Ceasar Chavez Center, and found Stafford Johnson, my advisor in the office of the Equal Education Opportunity Program. The entire staff of EEOP at Berkeley looked out for students like me. They were the people we went to whenever we needed help or guidance, when we just needed someone to talk to. Whenever we needed a place to feel welcomed or to feel like we belonged at Berkeley, we would go visit Stafford, Nate, and others. Well, Stafford was my advisor, so I went to see him.

I walked into his office, and told him what was going on. He immediately stood up, and said, "we need to fight this battle on an equal playing field. If you go back to your room, you are going to get lynched. But if you go to the police department to press charges against Robert, then we can put ourselves on the offensive position. Robert will then have to defend himself for attacking you." Sounded good to me.

Stafford escorted me and Johnny to the police station, took us to the receptionist area, and explained that we would like to file a police report against Robert for attacking me. The officer gave us forms, and Johnny and I spent about an hour explaining what had happened. We just wrote. Johnny wrote his eyewitness account of the incident, and I wrote mine.

Shortly after the incident, I got a letter in the mail informing me that I needed to visit the Office of Disciplinary Action, or something like that, because of the fight. Apparently, Robert's parents pulled some strings, and accused me of initiating the fight. However, because of Stafford's wisdom, and Johnny's written testimony about the incident, which substantiated my account, the charges against me were dismissed. As a relief to me, they ended up penalizing Robert for his misconduct.

People in Summer Bridge thanked me for shutting up Robert. I just shrugged my shoulders, like whatever. I was genuinely sorry that the whole thing happened. I just hoped he learned to talk to people with respect. All he had to do was ask Johnny, nicely, to turn the music down. The situation would have ended much more amicably.

Shortly after the incident, Robert transferred to UCLA.

Even though my fight against Robert was over, my fight at Berkeley was far from over. It was really just the beginning of my fight. Really, that fight was a metaphor for my entire academic experience at Berkeley. It set the tone for the remaining 5 years. What worked in the streets of Long Beach were not as helpful in the halls of Berkeley. I was going to have to learn how to fight less with my hands, and more with my mind.

37

In fall of 1995, about three weeks before Berkeley's fall semester, I moved into my new dorm room. I think my room number was 201. Since I moved in first, I picked which of the 3 beds I wanted. There were 3 beds, one of them had a lower bunk and a top bunk, while the other bunk had a desk where the lower bunk would normally be, and a bed above the desk. I picked the only lower bunk, and unpacked my bags.

After getting settled in, I decided to relax a bit. So I laid down in my bed, wearing only boxer shorts and a cut off grey shirt from football practice. I heard someone trying to put a key in the door. I figured that it was probably one of my new roommates. I didn't have time to put on any clothes, but felt the need to stand up, to answer the door just in case it was someone else. In walked a skinny Asian guy, his father, mother, and little sister. As soon as they saw me, they all backed up against the wall, like they were afraid of me. I thought it was kind of funny, so I tried to make it easier on them by introducing myself.

My roommate told me that his name was Johan, but he pronounced it as "Yo-hawn." I asked him where he was from. He came straight from Tokyo, Japan. Really, he and his family had just gotten off the airplane from Tokyo, and came straight to the dorm room. "Johan? Isn't that a Swedish name or something? Aren't you supposed to have blonde hair and be able to yodel if your name is Johan? You're from Tokyo. I just smiled.

That had to be the most incompatible name I had ever heard. It did not fit him. I found it really kind of funny, but I didn't say anything about it. In any case, I was sure that "Johan" was much easier to pronounce than his real Japanese name, whatever it was.

After his parents left, and he got settled in, he picked the bunk that was above the desk. I really wanted to learn a little bit more about Johan, especially because he and his family had backed up against the wall when they saw me. I had to ask.

"Johan, have you ever seen any black people before?"

"Two time," he said as he looked away.

"In Tokyo, you saw two black people in your city?"

"No. Two time," he said. "One time in Menace to Society. And in Boyz in the Hood." I just laughed. It all made sense now. Both of those movies depict the life of inner-city youth in Los Angeles who are involved in gangs. So Johan and his family were scared because they thought I was going to rob them or something! I just laughed. He laughed too, kind of nervously, as though he wasn't sure that I was any different from the guys he had seen in the movies.

Despite our language and cultural differences, Johan seemed really cool. It was fascinating: a brotha from Long Beach, CA living with a guy from Japan named Johan. We were from two different worlds.

A day later, my next roommate walked in. He was a white guy wearing a Minnesota Twins baseball cap. He wore a flannel shirt, and some hiking boots. His hair was light brown, he had a thin bird-like nose, and he was very pale. He had two front teeth that were slightly crooked when he smiled. He looked like he hadn't seen much sun.

He came in while Johan was away, so it was just me and Jim. We talked while he unpacked his luggage. I was trying to be polite, and open minded about being roommates with a white guy.

Jim told me he was from Minneapolis, Minnesota. I was like, "Cool. What's it like up there?"

He said, "Well, only two percent of the population is black, but they commit over 50 percent of the crime."

I was a little taken aback by his response. Why would that be the first thing he wanted to tell me about Minnesota? What did that have to do with his experience of the city?

"Oh, I get it. He doesn't really trust black people," I figured. But I had to ask, "Are you sure your numbers are correct?"

"Absolutely," he said emphatically.

After that brief, laconic exchange, the conversation ended. We both laid on our beds. Not talking.

I could already tell that living with Jim and Johan was going to be a challenge. I had to live in a room with a Japanese guy who thought I was going to rob him, and a white guy who was convinced that one out of every two black people in Minneapolis in particular, and probably everywhere else, are criminals.

The stereotype and stigma of being a black man on a college campus, in America, and probably around the world, is frustrating to say the least. No matter what I did to ingratiate myself to them, they, and several of their friends and families, were convinced they had me, and everyone who shared my complexion, figured out.

38

The profiling didn't just happen in my own dorm room; it spilled over into the classroom, among the Berkeley students too.

I enrolled in a class related to Urban Enclaves, and as usual, I was the only black person in the class. A few days into the class, the discussion turned to the subject of unemployment in the black community. Because I was the only black person in the class, felt that question personally. That question was not just an academic one for me. It was personal.

The professor asked, "why do you think the unemployment rate is so high among African American men?"

I felt like every spotlight in the world was shining on me. I was paralyzed. That question hit so close to home that I didn't even know how to talk about it in a theoretical, academic way. However, others were less reticent. While sitting there, a white guy spoke up. He said, "the reason that the unemployment rate is so high among black men is because black men are lazy. They don't want to work."

My blood began to boil. My jaw tightened. My fists balled up. My brow creased. I wanted to jump out of my seat and beat the living daylights out of him. I wanted to show him exactly how lazy black men were. In my heart, I knew why a lot of black men had it hard but I couldn't put into words. I didn't know all about slavery and its lasting effects on the black community; I didn't know about systemic racism, or about a welfare system that divided black families because it would not give financial help to families that had a father in the home, even if he couldn't find work; I didn't know how the black community had been castrated by a corrupted criminal justice system; I didn't know about how most black communities had unequal access to quality education and jobs; I didn't know about Brown versus The Board of Education or Plessy versus Ferguson or Jim Crow or disenfranchisement or the KKK. Although I didn't know about those things on an academic level, I grew up in places, around people, who were victims of all of those things. So it was just part of our DNA, but no one ever really talked about those things explicitly. It was just part of the culture. My culture of being black and brown in America.

In any case, I was pissed off. How dare he call black men lazy! I was so angry that I could not speak. All I wanted to do was fight. I wanted to kick his behind for saying that crap. I wanted to explode from being unable to defend my brothers, and my community, verbally. I wanted to cry out for my people. I wanted to explain why things were hard for so many of us. I wanted to explain that we did not have an equal playing field in America. I wanted to explain that the deck had been stacked against us. I wanted to explain to them that black people had been maimed and crippled for centuries. But my entire being was trembling to speak, but I just couldn't find the words to say.

I knew that if I opened my mouth, I would have probably said something that led to me beating him up.

Fortunately, some other students disagreed with him, and described some of the historic causes that had resulted in black men being unemployed. Even though I was a little relieved that others spoke up, I was still pissed off.

When class was over, I was the first one to leave. I rushed toward the door, with steam coming out of my ears. I hurried away because I didn't want to put my hands on him. I also rushed away because I was so pissed off at myself. "Why didn't I say something? Why didn't I speak up? How could I allow someone to say something like that and they go unchallenged or unpunished?" I beat myself up pretty bad for that.

I had some teachers who were just as ignorant as the guy who thought black men were lazy. I visited one of my teacher's office hours in order to start off the semester on the right foot. She was a graduate student, and Teachers Assistant, in the Political Science department. I walked into her office, and she didn't even smile when I entered. I took a seat next to her desk, and I tried to establish rapport with her. I tried to break the ice. I tried to use some of my charm to make a connection with her. None of it worked.

She asked me bluntly, "why did you enroll in this class?"

"Because I am interested in learning about politics and our political system," I explained.

Before I could really finish my response, she cut me off. "Do you have any questions about the material or the readings?"

"I am just a little new to reading this kind of stuff, and I'm a little nervous about starting off on the right foot. I want to make sure I learn-"

"You're an athlete, aren't you?" I didn't understand what that had to do with anything. I didn't tell her I walked onto the football team. I didn't tell her that I fought my way into Berkeley like most other students. I just looked at her for a second, startled.

She didn't ask me if I was an athlete to seek more information about me; it was clear, from her tone of voice, that she wanted to confirm a conclusion she had made about me before I ever uttered a word.

She had already written me off. She already doubted that I deserved to be at UC Berkeley. She didn't know that I was not on an athletic scholarship, but that I walked onto the team. Still, that had nothing to do with my visit. I got into Berkeley by working hard like everybody else. How dare she dismiss me like that? Before I ever thought about uttering a word, I felt a pressure to have to prove that I was as smart and able as everyone else at Berkeley.

As a black male, that kind of profiling and prejudice followed me everywhere I went. Whenever I walked into a convenience store, the clerks behind the counters always looked at my hands first, and then my face, as though they were looking for a gun. The fear in their eyes made it painfully clear that they were afraid I was going to rob them. When I walked into class, I could see people staring at me in the corner of their eyes, studying me. When I caught them and tried to kindly acknowledged them, they often ignored me.

Those experiences vexed me, and served as a wake up call for me. They fueled my flame to learn how to fight with my mind! I had to learn to fight with my words. I had to learn to summon the English language and send it forth into battle. I had to become a voice for the voiceless. If I don't speak for them, who will? I am one of them. I understand their pain. I understand their struggles. I understand poverty. I understand despair. I understand what it feels like to be trapped in misery.

39

Not only did everyone else doubt me, I started to doubt myself too. I was enrolled in Rhetoric 1b. There wasn't anyone from Summer Bridge in any of my classes, and, with the exception of Afro 1A, one of my other classes, I was the only African-American in all of my classes.

As I looked around, I could tell that everyone else in the class was white, very proper, and probably came from middle and upper class backgrounds. The way they contributed to class discussions was very impressive, and intimidating. The way they grappling with ideas, and thought on their feet, and advanced the conversation, and debated, was very intimidating. I started feeling like I did in middle and high school. I started feeling inadequate. I start feeling very self-conscious.

So I did not really participate in class discussions. The teacher tried to encourage "others" to join in on discussions about the ideas we are reading about in books, but when her encouragement fell on deaf ears, she informed us that thirty percent of our grade would be based on class participation. I was terrified, and I didn't know what to do! "How am I going to speak up? If I speak up, I might sound stupid. I might make a fool out of myself."

Unlike others in that class, I knew that I didn't have the luxury of getting to speak for myself. No! When I spoke, I spoke for every other black person in the world, in the minds of many of my white classmates. If I sounded stupid, I was going to confirm what many of those white people thought about black people- that we are ignorant. If

I didn't say anything, I was going to get a bad grade. If I did say something, it might have helped my grade, but it might also destroy my self-esteem. I didn't know how to participate in a class discussion as well as my other classmates. I hadn't learned how to communicate in academic settings of that caliber.

I had two problems. One, I had a hard time keeping up with the readings, because I didn't really know how to study for college-level coursework. Yes, I had made a great deal of improvement in high school, but not good enough to compensate for all of the school I missed through the years.

I also had a very hard time comprehending the material I read. Both of those problems came to a head one night when I went to a Barnes and Noble bookstore to study like I'd seen others do. I took my readings from class, and I was supposed to read the first chapter of Aristotle's Poetics. I sat down at a table, opened the book, and I started trying to read the very first paragraph. I read through it, and I stopped. I re-read it, trying to make more sense of what he was saying, but it was still unclear to me. I made it to the end of the paragraph, and I stopped reading, again.

"Maybe if I read it more slowly, just to get a better sense of the context of the paragraph, and what he's saying, I might understand this a little more," I hoped. I re-read the paragraph again, and I drew a blank.

Obviously, there were some words in the paragraph that I didn't understand, so I pulled out my dictionary and whenever I stopped at an unfamiliar word, I looked it up in the dictionary, and wrote the definition down in the book's margins. I started reading at the beginning of the paragraph again, and found another unfamiliar word, and I tried to make sense of what Aristotle was talking about. I mentally plugged in each new definition into the sentence, but I still did not understand what Aristotle was talking about.

I encountered the next hard word, defined it in the margins, and started over. I still didn't understand. I did that again and again: read a new word, defined it, and tried to read the sentence again by replacing the word with the definition, just so I could make sense of what was going on in the text.

After 5 hours of me doing that, the margins around the paragraph were completely blackened with definitions. However, I still did not understand what the paragraph was about.

It was about 11pm and the store was about to close, and I still didn't get it. My frustration turned to discouragement; and, my discouragement turned to self-pity. My heart and mind said in substance, "Maybe I'm not smart enough. Maybe I don't deserve to be here. Maybe I'm dumb!" I then concluded, " I can't do this. I've done my best. I've done everything I was told to do when I saw words I didn't understand, but I still have no clue what he's talking about."

I started crying. I put my head down on the desk so others wouldn't see me. The anger, the sadness, the self-doubt. I wondered, "What's wrong with me? Why can't I get this? I am going to fail this class."

I started seriously thinking about what kind of jobs I could get if I moved back to Long Beach. I started thinking about calling my friend back who offered me a job working with his uncle at a garage. He said I could answer phones and do some filing.

But then I somehow started thinking about mom, and Alex, and all the cops who mistreated me. I started thinking about the times I was almost killed. I started thinking about Malcolm X's story, and about the slaves who, years ago, in cramped slave shacks, prayed that one day their children would be free. They struggled and died for me to be able to go to school. They were lynched for me to be there. Their families were torn apart for me to be here. If I give up now, their sacrifices were in vain.

"I can't give up now! I must keep fighting. I am not a quitter. God, you didn't save me from all the things I've been through to leave me out here now. You didn't bring me through all of that to leave me here alone. God, please help me! I need your help! Lord, please make it plain for me. Please help me to understand. Please help me. Give me the courage to speak in class. Help me, please!"

That night, I made up my mind that I would fight to catch up. I would fight to stay at Berkeley. I would fight to prove that I could succeed.

The next day, I went to class, and the teacher opened the class with a question about the readings. Not knowing really anything, I just blurted out something that made no sense whatsoever. But I did it. I said something. Then others jumped in. I didn't say anything else for the rest of the class, but I sat their with pride. I said something!

I still knew in my heart though, that I had a lot of work to do in order to compensate for all those years of missed school. But it felt good to say something. Baby steps!

40

But something was missing. I felt like a fish out of water in a sense. Berkeley helped me see that I didn't really know a whole lot about who I was as a person, and I knew even less about Black history.

So I enrolled in Afro 1A, Introduction to African American Studies. With the isolation I felt in all my other classes, it was nice to be around other people who looked like me, who understood me, at least a little, and who didn't judge me. Also, I was excited to be able to take a class that related to me and my history. In high school, I never had the option to take classes that taught me about black history, because there were none offered. Before college, the only thing I had ever read about black people in my history books was found in one paragraph, and it said that black people were slaves or something like that. That was it! People who looked like me were slaves. There was never any information about the history of black people before the Transatlantic slave trade. And the only person who had done anything important, according to my history book, was the Rev. Dr. Martin Luther King.

So, to say the least, I was excited about the opportunity to learn a little bit more about black culture and black people.

The professor was Omowale Fowles. She was a woman who wore African kente cloths, head scarves, and a whole lot of other stuff. Her outfits became punchlines among black students. People said when she woke up in the morning, she put on everything she had in her closet, at the same time. She was a peculiar woman, but a very smart woman, for whom I give great thanks.

She talked about how important it was for us, as African-American students, to succeed at the University of California at Berkeley. She lectured us about Willie Lynch, Slavery, oppression.

She emphasized the importance of understanding latin prefixes and suffixes, and assigned all kinds of vocabulary exercises to us in order to help us develop our ability to express ourselves.

She gave us the option of reading Malcolm X's autobiography or Assata Shakur's autobiography. I chose Malcolm X.

That book lit a fire in me like no other book had. It talked so honestly, and in my opinion, accurately, about many of the white people I had met. His journey from being a street hustler to becoming El Hajj Al-Malik El-Shabazz, or better known as Malcolm X, kept me captivated. I found some of my own life in his story. I understood some of my own anger through his words. It was very powerful for me to finally connect with an author who understood me.

I could not put the book down. When he talked about his studies in prison, I felt so inspired. I reasoned, " if someone like Malcolm X could come from the streets, and master language so well, then I can too." I had always wanted to use words well, but Malcolm really fired me up to learn more of them.

I started carrying around a dictionary to help me learn, and understand, unfamiliar words. When I was reading a book, and came across a word I didn't understand, I pulled out my dictionary, found the word, and then wrote its definition in the margins of the book. In that way, I began to grow my vocabulary.

The class discussions were exhilarating. If only all my classes were like that.

During one of my classes, Omowale Fowles brought in Harry Edwards to talk to the class about sports and black athletes. Dr. Edwards spoke eloquently about the way sports often exploited black students, made millions of dollars off of college athletes, and never really took the time to care about the education or the long-term well-being of those athletes. He told me that if I played sports, to make sure I did not put all my eggs in the football basket, because it is very unlikely that I, or most college athletes, would become professional athletes.

Harry Edwards challenged the class to do our homework on the lives of former professional black athletes. I was the only athlete in the class, so I was absolutely convinced that Omowale Fowles brought Dr. Edwards in for me.

As a result of that class, I actually spent a couple days in the library researching black athletes, and I discovered that of the tiny percentage of black athletes who had made it to the professional level, their careers often ended after 3 years, on average. And ten years after their careers were over, a staggering fifty percent or something, ended up broke, and sometimes homeless. I remember reading that and being blown away by it. I did not do anything about it when I read it, but that research, and Dr. Edwards' presentation, returned to my mind several times in the days and months ahead.

Afro 1A was the only class where I felt validated. I felt like I belonged. I felt like I mattered. It was the only class where I began to realize the importance of my history, and the history of black people in America, and Africa.

By taking that class, I felt like I was learning more about me. I felt like someone had lied to me all my life. Mom told me I was black when I was five, but nobody ever talked positively about what that meant. Nobody ever told me about the importance of knowing my history, and about what people who looked like me had accomplished in history.

That class gave me a sense of pride that I did not really have before. I became more curious about my own roots. About my own family.

I began wondering more about my father. Who was he? Where was he? How was he doing? Was he still alive? Has he been looking for me? Has he been trying to find me? What he's like? What has his life been like? Why did he leave, really? Who was his father? Who was his mother? Why haven't I had any connection with his family, if there is one? Who am I? What difference does it make that I know him? What difference does it make that I am black, in America?

41

Early into my first semester of college, I received a letter from Raymond Grate, my biological father. I stared at the letter for a moment to make sure I was not seeing things. I didn't know what to think. I hurried upstairs to my room, and was glad to see I had the room to myself. I dropped my things, and read the envelope again to see from where my father sent the letter. The number next to his name, and the address, indicated that he was incarcerated at a prison in Nevada. I opened the letter and sat on the edge of my bed.

He greeted me with a biblical greeting. His handwriting was in cursive, but very neat. He told me that he found my mother, and she gave him my address. He told me that he was proud of me, and he also said not a day had gone by since I was five years old that he did not think of me or pray for me and my mother. He expressed regret for being absent from most of my life. Then he mentioned he would be getting out pretty soon, and that he would like to stay in touch with me. He said he wanted to get to know me. He asked me to write him back when I had time because he would love to hear from me. He also asked for my phone number because he would call me, if I was okay with it.

I had mixed emotions about the letter. A part of me was happy to hear from him; another part of me was very hesitant to trust him and let him into my life. I figured, "what do I have to lose? Give it a try."

Because I had been wanting to know more about my own history, I thought it was important to at least try to develop a relationship with him. Growing up, to rationalize my father's absence, I used to always say, "you never miss what you never had." Well, the fact was, I did miss some things with my father being gone: I didn't learn how to shave until I got to college. I didn't learn how to tie a tie, until my sophomore year; I didn't learn how to carry myself, or how to treat women the right way, or how to relate to other men who were older than I was- there was a lot I missed.

To be sure, my mom did the best she could to raise boys on her own. I used to send mom father's day cards, because she was the only dad I really knew. But there were some things I needed to get and learn from a man. Manuel, my step-father when I was a child, never called for my birthdays. He never sent cards, he never just called to say hello. After he and mom separated, I did not hear from him again for years, unless I reached out to him. Whenever he did call our house, he would say hi to me if I answered the phone, but within seconds, he asked to talk to my mom. If she wasn't available, he got off the phone quickly. As I grew older, I understood why he didn't do any of those things. After all, I was not his biological son. Still, to a kid who knew no one other than him as my dad, I took it kind of hard.

So, when my father took the initiative to reach out to me, I saw it as a chance to really get to know him, and perhaps more about myself. What attributes and idiosyncrasies of his do I have, if any? I put his letter in my backpack, and headed out to the stadium for football practice.

Over the next several months, my father and I talked on the phone. It was kind of cool getting to know him. His voice sounded the same as I remembered it when I was five years old. Eventually, he was released from prison in Nevada, and moved to Denver, Colorado.

Mom and I flew to Colorado to spend Thanksgiving with Grandma, my brothers and the rest of the family. On Thanksgiving day, people came from all over. My brothers arrived from Sterling with Grandma. Aunt Gloria came with her boyfriend, Beto and Bruno showed up too. Mara arrived with her boyfriend, and Martha showed her face. Everyone was there, eating, and enjoying Grandma's cooking, like the good old days.

I was catching up with my brothers and cousins. We went outside to play catch with the football, and talk about old times, when I saw my father walking toward us in the distance. I started walking toward my father, with a smile on my face. I threw the football at him in the distance. He caught it, and threw it back. It wobbled through the air. It had to be one of the ugliest throws I have ever seen in my life.

I hugged him; he squeezed me, much like he did when I was five. I was almost as tall as him. He hadn't aged that much. He was still very slender, but he had a little less hair on his head. The years had obviously taken their toll on him, but he still looked well for his age.

We walked toward the house where he saw and hugged mom. They exchanged niceties. It was neat to see mom light up. They had a connection that I'd never seen mom have before. He was the only man that mom had ever truly loved. I'd always hear her say that, but seeing her with my father allowed me to see it with my own eyes. It was kind of nice to see my mom and my father together, catching up.

After several minutes of talking, he asked if I wanted to go for a walk. Sure. We walked, and talked, and I learned a lot about his life. He said his mother was not a very nice person. She used to beat him. She once put rat poison in his food when he was younger, but he caught her in the act. He ran away from home at the age of 16, and had to fend for himself on the streets of Denver. He taught himself Jeet Koon Du, Bruce Lee's style of martial arts.

I asked him why he went to prison, and told me about how it all started. He used to steal to survive, and got better and better at it. He used to get adrenaline rushes whenever he committed crimes.

My father burglarized so many businesses that he became known as Denver's infamous "Rooftop Bandit." He used to find an opening in the roof, and lower himself down into stores. He did that for years.

When I asked him how he finally got caught, he said, at one of the locations, he lowered himself into the store, and a female security guard showed up. Although he could have hurt her, he said he could never hit a woman. So he froze, and let her arrest him.

I'm not sure if that's why he left me when I was 5 years old, but it was a fascinating story to hear. Since I was going to be in Denver a few more days, I figured we had a little more time to spend getting to know each other. It was just nice to talk. We talked until evening, and made plans to hang out the next day.

The next day, he took me to his job, and showed me how he supervised over 100 employees at a call center in Denver's pac-man building. He was smart, and very articulate. Talking to him, you would have never known that he had been in prison for almost all of his adult life. He was poised, charming, polite, and very loving. He told me that he did not have any more children because he did not want anymore children. He said he only had me, and he was happy.

He walked around, boasting to random people that I was his son. We ate, laughed, and talked. He told me more about his comedy, about his bad temper, and his quirks. It was gratifying to hang out with him.

In the restaurant we went into, the Aloha Bowl was on TV, and Cal was playing against someone. I would have been there, but I had a confrontation with a coach that led me to reevaluate my priorities about football.

42

With a friend's encouragement, I decided to try out for the Young Inspiration Gospel Choir on campus, which was led by Sylvester Henderson. Sylvester, a fun disciplinarian, with a big presence. Bald headed, brown skin, and a black beard, with glasses that sat on his nose, low enough so he could peak over them at you to give you that look that parents give you when you are out of line. He had braces around his wrist to help him with his carpal tunnel. He spoke with a slight lisp, and a quick, stacatto pace to his words.

Sylvester sat me in the tenor section, and occasionally selected me to sing solos for the concerts. Every friday night from 6:30-9:30, we rehearsed with Sylvester. It was a great time, full of fun, singing, and friendship development.

It was there that I met Jon Decuir, the prodigy pianist from Pasadena, California. Jon was a year older than I was, but played piano like no one I had ever heard. He hit chords in ways I didn't think were possible. They were what we called "sick," because they needed a doctor.

I spent a lot of time in choir. Before rehearsal, Jon and I often had bible study, which was led by a guy named Evan. Other days, I attended a bible study led by Andy Fitzgerald for Athletes in Action. It was a great time of growing in my faith.

Singing in the choir and the solos helped me get more comfortable being on stage in front of people. It was in choir that I really gained an appreciation for gospel music. I learned about Fred Hammond, the Winans, Kirk Franklin, and other gospel greats.

It was in the choir that I learned to sing, "If I Can Help Somebody," a song that I often sing at the beginning of my presentations.

I loved singing, and for a time, thought I was going to become a singer like Boys II Men, but I didn't have the skill or gifting to sing like the people I admired. I could hold a note, and emulate others, but could not really sang. I did not know how to sing like those who interpret songs, and tell their stories in the way that great singers do.

There were times when I felt that my singing was inspired, and helped a lot of people, but I did not think that that was my primary calling. I still wasn't sure what that was yet.

Something that happened around this time, though, helped me get closer to finding out what I was born to do.

Shortly after my father and I reconnected, a friend, Nicky Hogan, who was over the Black Recruitment and Retention Center's Retention program, asked me if I would host showtime at the Apollo on campus. I was hesitant because I had never been on stage before as a host or an MC before. Yeah, I was always clowning around, and telling jokes, but I had never officially been the guy responsible to engage an audience, help them have fun, all while keeping the event flowing.

It was the thrill seeker in me, combined with the confidence I inherited from momma, that inspired me to take on new challenges. I knew I could blow it, but I also felt like I could do well too. So I agreed to serve as the MC of the event.

To prepare for the event, I figured I needed some help. Well, who better to help me than my father, a former stand-up comedian? He stood on stages and woo'd audiences. I'd seen him do it with my own eyes. He moved them to laughter, and charmed them, and gave them great memories. Maybe he could help me do the same thing.

I gave him a call, and told him I needed his help. Would he help me? Where do I start? What do I need to know? How do I make people laugh?

He calmed my nerves, and coached me through it. He told me how to open, and different ways to introduce people, and ways to engage the audience. And he said, the most important part is that I remember, if it is funny to me, then it will be funny to the audience. But if it is not truly funny to me, then don't say it, and don't do it. He said that I already had great timing, and great instincts. All I needed to do was rehearse and be myself.

The night of the event came, and I got dressed. I didn't know how to tie a tie, but Jared, my roommate taught me.

The people started filing into Dwinelle Hall, and the room filled to capacity. The DJ played music to set the tone.

The time came for me to get the party started. I was nervous, but excited. I walked on stage, grabbed the mic, and welcomed everyone to Showtime at the Apollo. I opened with a joke. "I got to tell you guys this. I'm a little nervous. The last time I stood in front of this many people, I was in a lineup." They laughed. I laid the ground rules, and then introduced the first guest. She did well. I introduced the second guest, and she didn't do so well. The audience let her know by booing her off the stage. It was all in good fun, though.

In between performers, I had to fill time with jokes, with improvising, thinking on my feet, keeping the audience engaged. I had an absolute blast, and the people loved it! Afterwards, people came up to me, shook my hand, and thanked me for making the event such a great experience.

I had never felt so at home in my life. Telling jokes, having fun with an audience. I was a natural. I felt so fulfilled by the work.

I couldn't wait to talk to my father, to thank him for all his help, and tell him how great things had gone. Unfortunately, I never got the chance to do that.

43

On the next day, when I returned home after class, I walked into my bedroom, I checked my voicemail. It was my father. He was sad.

He said, "Hello son, it's me, dad…Son, I messed up again." I could hear him crying. "I'm calling you from the back of a police van. I messed up again son…I'll be going away for a long time. I'm so sorry, son. I pray you will one day be able to forgive me. I'm so sorry son. I love you so much. I am so proud of you. I love you son. Goodbye."

I stood there, numb. Jared walked into my room, and he saw me standing there. "He asked me, "what's wrong?"

I couldn't even answer. I just started crying. I told him about my father's message. He gave me a hug.

"Aw man. I'm sorry, dogg. Damn! I'm sorry dogg!" Jared said.

After we talked for a few minutes, Jared left, I closed my door, I turned off my light, and I just laid in bed and shed a few tears.

It was one of the most difficult moments in my life. My heart was completely open to my father. I let him in. I gave him a chance, and trusted him. We were getting close, and I was beginning to heal from his absence. Things were going great, I thought, and my life was getting much better. But his voicemail broke me down.

With tears in my eyes, I laid on that bed wondering, "How could he do this to me? How could he leave me hanging like this, again? Forget him! I will never trust him, or anyone else again. I'll never let anyone else in. I'm done trusting people. It's not worth it. The pain was too deep. The sadness was too heavy. I just could not take that kind of disappointment again. I ached in the depths of my soul.

44

Near then end of our football season in the fall of 1995, things became clear for me that my football days were coming to an end. We had just lost a game to the Arizona, and Coach Taylor the wide receivers coach revealed his true colors. He berated the receivers for a mediocre performance, challenged the starters, pointing out their mistakes, missed blocks, misread coverages, bad routes, dropped balls, penalties, hustle, and so on.

He then told us our reason and purpose for playing football: "Your job is to help me keep my job. That's it! Do whatever you have to do in school. That's not my problem. That's your problem. Your job is simply this: to help me keep my job."

While I hated losing, and I understood he hated losing too, I could not understand why he cared so little about us as people. He could not have cared less about our grades, and our families, and our futures. All he cared about was winning, even if it meant that we, the student-athletes, lost individually in the long run.

I looked down at my daily schedule:
Football Practice from 5:30 A.M.-7:30 A.M.;
Classes from 8 A.M.-2 P.M.
Lift Weights from 2 P.M.-3 P.M.
Position Meeting from 3 P.M.-4 P.M.
Practice from 4:30 P.M. −7:30 P.M.
Dinner from 7:30 P.M. to 8 P.M.
Study Hall 8:15 P.M.- 10 P.M.

With a schedule like that, I was too tired to read, too tired to do research, and too tired to do quality work. Maybe that schedule worked for other guys who had better study habits before they went to college. Nonetheless, it didn't work for me. I had a lot of catching up to do. I had a lot of reading to do. I actually wanted to learn, to be sharpened. But the fact was, I was not doing my best academically.

Then Dr. Harry Edwards's words to me in my Afro 1A class were breathed upon my remembrance. He warned me about putting football over school. He helped me see that I was just a cog in a wheel. We, as athletes, were only as good as our bodies were to their system. Some of our coaches wanted to use us up, and throw us away. Yes, we needed to win; but we also needed to look at the bigger picture of our development as men, and future fathers, as future husbands, as people of character and integrity. We needed to be able to get jobs. Our community needed us. We needed to represent.

In that moment, I decided that I was not going to put all my eggs in the football basket anymore. I just wasn't feeling passionate about football anymore. The politics, the personalities, the schedule, the twisted priorities. I lost my love for the game. I didn't study my playbook like I should have. My priorities had changed.

Shortly after that, the team made it into the Aloha Bowl against the Navy, and the team was about 2 weeks away from going to Hawaii. While I was in the locker room, getting dressed, coach Hue Jackson sat down next to me and told me that I was not going to be going to Hawaii with the team. While I calmly disagreed with him, I knew in my heart that it was okay. I thought Coach Taylor was a coward for asking Jackson to break the news to me, but then again, it didn't surprise me. That conversation sealed the deal for me. I was done. It was time to hang up my cleats.

Sometimes you have to say goodbye to the things you love because it's time. Life is a season of partings, punctuated, if we are fortunate, by moments of great joy. Football provided me great joy. It was all I ever wanted to do when I was a little boy. Now, it was over. I had the privilege of playing with Tony Gonzalez, the future Hall of Fame Tight End. We actually sat next to each other in the locker room. He used to call me "Song Bird" because I was always singing. I had the privilege of playing under Steve Marriucci, one of the most charismatic coaches I'd ever seen. I was able to make friends with some really amazing guys. So leaving the team was a bittersweet, but it was necessary.

Interestingly enough, after my departure from the team, the team went on a 4-year losing streak; and, the Cal football program was chastised because the players barely had a graduation rate of 48 percent, ranking Cal last in the Pac-12. As I look back, I know I made the right decision to leave the team, even though it was hard. I wasn't good enough to make that big of a difference on the team, and I was no longer willing to sacrifice an education at one of the best universities in the world for football.

With football out of the picture I had time to begin finding an identity outside of football. I found it in one of Berkeley's 55 libraries.

45

After quitting the football team, I had more time to devote to other pursuits. I read the autobiography of Frederick Douglass and I was so inspired by his tenacity to learn to read. In his book he talked about reading the Columbian Orator and memorized speeches out of it. I figured that I would do that too. In my empty room, I started reciting speeches and poems out of that book.

The words I read awakened in me a fire to learn more. I began to read about Dr. King, and the Montgomery Bus Boycott. I learned about Rosa Parks and the Montgomery Improvement Association. I learned about the Albany Movement, the Birmingham Movement, and the March from Selma to Montgomery; I internalized Dr. King's Letter from the Birmingham Jail; I mourned over the 4 little girls who were murdered in Birmingham, Alabama; I wept over the murders of Ms. Viola Liuzzo, Schwerner, Goodman, and Cheney. I journeyed with the Black Panthers, Stokely Carmichael, SNCC, and the Urban League, the NAACP; I internalized the March on Washington, and marched mentally with sanitation workers in Memphis; I dreamed of joining the War on Poverty in which people from all over the country would occupy our nation's capitol for poor people everywhere.

I drank deeply from their works, and wrestled with their ideas about justice, sacrifice, service; I recited their speeches in an empty room. I was moved in a way that I had never been moved. I felt as though I was finding my voice through reading, and listening to the voice of others who fought for people like me. They sacrificed, marched, were beaten, castrated, lynched, and died so that I could have the rights and privileges of other Americans.

I changed my role models from athletes to people who actually used their lives to help others in need. Those were the true heroes and role models who deserved to be venerated and emulated. I loved sports for all my life, but I did not see any athletes standing up for anyone other than themselves. I didn't see anyone standing for the least, the last, the lost, or left out.

So I changed my role models. I put pictures of them up on my wall. Kids put posters of musicians and entertainers; I put up pictures of Dr. King, with his family; Malcolm X and his family; Nelson Mandela; and I looked at them whenever I needed a reminder about what really mattered. Whenever I forgot about why I was able to attend college, I looked at those pictures and read those books.

I read so much about the Civil Rights Movement that I began to dream about one day meeting Mrs. King, Mrs. Betty Shabazz, the Rev. Dr. Gardner C. Taylor, and Nelson Mandela, because I felt indebted to them, and I felt even more determined to become a voice for the voiceless. I wanted to become a lawyer.

Then one of my dreams came true, the day I met Mrs. King. Around that time, I went to Atlanta for spring break with my roommate, Aaron Smith. Aaron had a friend in Atlanta named Richard, and said we could stay at Rich's house.

In Atlanta, the guys did what many college guys do in Atlanta. Driving around, going to different campuses to pick up women, and get numbers, and have a good time. While I went along for the ride, I was really trying to go spend some time alone in downtown Atlanta so I could visit sites that I had read about during my studies on the Civil Rights Movement.

I went to the King Center and saw his robe, his bible, his marching boots, his Nobel Peace Prize, and his briefcase. I visited Ebenezer Baptist church, and sat in the pews in which people sat and heard Dr. King preach. Sermons were being played in the sanctuary, and I just sat there, being inspired again by his words.

I walked down to the SCLC offices, and the staff invited me in and let me have a tour of the office where Dr. King and staff met. They let me sit at the table where the movement was planned. I sat in the same seat, at the same table that Dr. King sat in. There was nothing special about the furniture or architecture of the room. It was special because of who worked there, and what was planned there.

Then I walked back over to the King Center, and was looking at the exhibits. The day was nearly over, but I wanted to watch every video, and read every display and see every exhibit. I slowly walked through the museum when a security guard walked up to me, and told me that the center was closed. I apologized to him, and thanked him. I headed out the door when he called me back. He whispered to me, "would you like to meet Mrs. King?"

Are you kidding me? Would I like to meet Mrs. King? Of course I'd like to meet Mrs. King! He escorted me through the building, to a door. He opened the door, and told me to go right in. I walked into the room, and there she was, Mrs. King. "Corrie" as Dr. King called her. She was standing at a lectern, as regal and beautiful as ever. She was queenly in her disposition. There were only about twenty people in the room.

Without really thinking, I walked all the way to the front of the room, and sat in the very front row, maybe four feet from her. As I looked back, I probably startled her a little bit because I sat so close to her, but she handled my alacrity so graciously.

She discussed a book about King and Ghandi. She talked about Dr. King. But she referred to him as "Marty." Marty?! She didn't call him Dr. King; she called him Marty. I was so honored to be sitting in her presence, listening to her words. I don't really remember everything she talked about, because it was kind of a blur, but I'll never forget how in awe I was to be in her presence.

She finished speaking, and I sat there in awe. I waited in line to meet her and shake her hand. She was sitting down, and her manager told us that Mrs. King would not be taking pictures that day. I got to the front of the line, and I mumbled something like, "Mrs. King, I am so honored to meet you. I am speechless. I want to thank you for all you have done to keep Dr. King's legacy and dream alive."

She looked at me and said, "you're so welcome." She grabbed my right hand and held it. She looked me in the eyes, and said, "he did it for you." I didn't know what to say. She thanked me, and I moved on. I walked out the doors, into the lobby, and I just stood there in shock.

What could she have possibly meant when she said that he did it for me? I wasn't even alive when Dr. King lived. He was murdered in 1968 and I was born in 1977. He did it for me? Then, in that moment, I recalled one of his speeches where he says, "one of these days people will look back at this time and know that I was fighting for the privileges and opportunities for them. I am fighting for them and their children." Dr. King fought and marched for me, and for poor people, for the downtrodden, for the disenfranchised. He fought for me.

With goosebumps still standing on my arms. All that I had ever studied rushed through my veins to my heart and mind. Mrs. King, Dr. King, the civil rights leaders like Andrew Young, and many others, were not just people in a history book who had lived a long time ago. No, they were regular human beings, just like me, who gave their lives to a cause bigger than themselves. They were ordinary people who did extraordinary things. They fought for justice and equality. They sacrificed their own comforts for me and people like me.

On that day, I made up my mind. "That's what I want my life to be about. I want to be a servant. I want to make a difference. I want to do something like that too. When I become a lawyer, I'll be able to do just that." I reasoned.

That experience affected me in very profound ways.

Having met the widow of Dr. King, I thought of something he told her on their first date. He told her that he knew that she had all of the qualities of the kind of woman he would marry.

Meeting her made me think about the kinds of qualities I wanted my future wife to have.

46

Late one night of my first year of college, I was walking from my dorm room to Clark Kerr, to hang out with Devin Lonon, a friend and football player from Long Beach. While walking up a little hill behind building 17, I saw someone with a flashlight walking along the path behind the building. It was a young lady, wearing some light grey sweatpants, a grey sweatshirt with CAL logo on the front. I said, "hello."

She said, "hi." But it wasn't just a regular "hi;" it was the kind of greeting that arrests you- sweet, innocent, gracious, and very lady-like. She had a sweetness in her voice that made her sound so beautiful.

I walked a few more steps, and felt compelled to stop. "WHO WAS THAT?" I had been at Berkeley almost an entire year, and I knew most of the black students on campus, and yet I had never seen her before. She was beautiful. She had no make-up on her face, and was so gracious. She was a lady.

I needed to introduce myself to her. I needed to find out who she was. So I turned around, looking for her, but she was already gone. I couldn't let her get away, so I walked in the direction she was heading. When I got to the corner of the building where she must have turned, and she was no where in sight. Did she go into one of these buildings? Who was that? I walked around the building a little more and realized I had lost her. I gave up for the night, but I could not get that girl out of my head.

A few months later, some of the guys and I went to Showtime at the Apollo, which was being held in the large room of Dwinelle Hall. I sat in the front row, and watched the show. After the show, I looked around and greeted a bunch of friends. I saw several women in the room who looked great. As my boys and I got up to leave the show, I noticed her again. It was the same beautiful woman I crossed paths with at Clark Kerr's building 17.

I couldn't resist. I missed her once; I'm not gonna miss this chance again. I walked up the stairs to the row she was sitting in. She looked at me, smiling, and I introduced myself, "Hi, I'm Manny. What's your name?"

"Alice," she said.

"Hi Alice," I said, smiling. "I hardly ever see you around. What are you studying?"

"Chemistry," she said.

"Oh, so that's why I never see you. You're always studying!" I replied.

"Pretty much," she said, in that same sweet tone of voice that I first heard months before.

"Well, Alice. It's so nice to meet you. I hope to see you around sometime. Take care," I said, and then walked up the stairs and out the room to catch up with Devin and the guys.

For some reason, I didn't think to ask her for her phone number, and I kicked myself for that, because there was something really special about Alice. She wasn't like any girl I had ever met.

Around the time when I was becoming less passionate about football, and less satisfied with where I was mentally and emotionally in my life, my good friend Jon Decuir, from choir, invited me join him on a fast so we could seek God's will for our lives. I did. We agreed that we would not eat any food for seven days. All we could drink was water and juice.

Every day that week, I opened my Bible and read Matthew 6:33, which says, "Seek first the kingdom of God, and His righteousness, and all these things will be given to you." Every morning when I woke up, I prayed for God to give me clarity and illumination as I read the Bible. I read and prayed for insight and understanding about what I was reading. I prayed for my heart to be purified....I prayed, and genuinely sought God's will for my life, whatever it was.

Every day I prayed, and every day I felt spiritually stronger. Some things that I thought were important under normal circumstances became less important. Every day that I prayed, I felt closer and closer to God, and closer and closer to who God created me to be.

About four or five days into our fast, I was physically hungry, but spiritually full. While in prayer, I began to think about the long term vision of my life. I began to think about where I believed I was being called to go, and who I was being called to be. In those prayers, I literally began to see myself speaking to large audiences. I felt in my heart God was giving me glimpses of things to come. As I thought about serving Him, I had a very long view of the kind of person He wanted me to be. I wasn't exactly sure what that was yet, but I felt called to help other people. I felt called to speak to audiences, small and large.

That far into my fast, I wasn't interested anymore in the short-sighted pleasures that some women on campus made available so readily. I wasn't interested in sex, in partying, in superficial relationships. I wanted deep, meaningful, lasting relationships with people who were clear about their faith, and who loved God, and wanted to serve Him in the same manner I did. So during the prayer, I asked God to give me clarity about who He wanted me to partner with. I prayed something like, "Lord, if it be your will, please show me the person you created to come alongside me and join me in this work I feel you calling me to do." During that prayer, the Lord placed Alice on my heart. I didn't understand it. It came out of nowhere. It was a strong, compelling pressure on my heart. It was similar to the pressure I felt on that park bench when I met Martin Stevens, when he shared his faith with me, which I accepted. That same presence, that same pressure, or feeling, rested upon me, then filled my being, and compelled me with an unequivocal conviction that Alice was "the one."

I wrapped up my prayer, got off my knees, and sat on the edge of my bed, kind of surprised. Alice? Really? I only met her one time. She seemed very nice, and sweet, but Alice? I smiled, stood up, walked to the sink to wash my face, and got ready for class.

After class, I met up with Jon so we could talk and pray and read our bibles together. I told him that I asked God to show me who he wanted me to partner with as my partner in life for the things He wanted me to do. Without hesitating, Jon said, "You know who you need to talk to?"

"Who?" I asked with focused curiosity.

"Alice," he said. I thought to myself, "Alice? No way! God, there is no way Jon could have known that." I had never even mentioned Alice's name to Jon. And she hardly came down to the south side of campus, so how would he even know who she was, I wondered.

He continued, "She doesn't come out much, but she is brown skinned. She wears long skirts, even in the summer. She doesn't wear makeup, but she is the real deal.

She wears turtlenecks when it's hot outside, bro." I laughed. God confirmed through Jon that Alice was supposed to be my wife.

But where could I find her? She almost never came outside. God was going to have to make it possible.

Shortly after my fast, which took place around April of 1997, I decided to go to a play on campus because several of my friends were in the play. I took the BART train to campus. I was running a little late. I jogged to Zellerbach Hall, and entered the side of the building, and went downstairs to get to the lower level, where smaller theater productions took place. I turned the corner, and saw a long line of people waiting to buy their tickets. There had to be at least 50-60 people in front of me in that line. The theater was very small, holding maybe one hundred people, so it didn't look like I was going to get in. The person selling tickets stood up and announced, "we are full. We only have one ticket left. Is there anyone here who needs one ticket?"

I just knew someone else was going to raise their hand, so I didn't even bother. No one spoke up. The cashier repeated himself. I leaned out of the line, raising my hand, and said, "I'll take it." I rushed passed the line, paid $20 for my ticket, entered the dark theater. The play had already started, so I tipped quietly toward the usher who checked my ticket with a small flashlight, and walked me up the aisle to my row. I eased down the row and took my seat.

I saw several of my friends in the play. At intermission, someone got on the microphone and announced that we were free to take a 10-minute-break. The lights in the room were turned up, and I heard someone in front of me say, "Hi Manny!" I looked up, delightfully surprised. It was Alice.

"Hey, Alice! How are you?"

"I'm great."

"I never see you around," I said. In light of what had happened to me during my fast with Jon, I needed to figure out a way to not let that opportunity pass without me somehow getting Alice's phone number. Since I was going to be singing in a gospel choir concert in a couple weeks, I used that as my selling point. So I asked her, "You coming to the gospel choir concert?"

She said she had already been asked, but didn't plan on attending. I encouraged her to reconsider, telling her it would be fun. She said she didn't have tickets.

Smiling on the inside, I told her, "I think I can help you out with that." If you give me your number, I'll be glad to meet you somewhere to give them to you. They're $10 each. Instead of giving me her number, she asked for mine. I guess that would have to work.

She said, "I'll call you if I am able to make it."

"Okay, but don't wait too long. These tickets are going fast," I warned.

I gave her my number, and the lights began to dim. The show resumed. We ended our conversation, and I leaned back into my seat in disbelief about what had just taken place.

What are the chances that I would get the last ticket, to the last seat of a show, and sit right behind Alice, the girl who almost NEVER came to the southside of campus, the girl I believed was supposed to be my wife?

In that seat, for the rest of the play, trying to focus on the play, I sat in disbelief.

When the play ended, I again encouraged Alice to give me a call so she could get her tickets to the concert.

She smiled, with such a beautiful, kind smile, and said she would.

She walked away with her friend, and I with great delight.

A few weeks after meeting Alice at that play, the Young Inspiration Gospel Choir concert was approaching, and I was able to convince Alice to attend. I was looking forward to seeing Alice. She didn't know it yet, but she was supposed to be my wife.

The choir, processed into the church, and began singing our opening song. For two hours, we sang some really powerful gospel music. That night, I sang a duet with a friend named Guy Holloman, which went very well. It was truly one of the most powerful moments of my life. It seemed like another foreshadow of things to come.

The closing prayer was prayed, and everyone in the choir went their own way. Jon asked if I was going to be going to dinner with some of the members of the choir. Of course, but I wanted to see if Alice, who was in attendance, wanted to join us.

As I approached the stage, scanning the audience for Alice, another young lady approached me- one that I had at one point had feelings for- and she told me that she had been thinking a lot about me lately. On ANY other day before then, I would have jumped at the opportunity to explore the tone of her intentions. I could have seen myself marrying that girl at one point. But not anymore. Not that night.

The Lord had shown me my wife- Alice. And there she was, coming through the back door of the sanctuary. I guess she had left, but came back to see me. With a big grin on my face, and in my heart, I greeted her.

"Great job," she said.

"Thank you. Thanks for coming out. Did you enjoy yourself?"

"I did. It was great. You really hit that note. Thank you for inviting me."

I then tried to make my appeal. "A group of us are going out to dinner. You should come."

"Oh, thank you, but I can't," she said. "I'm here with a friend, and she's outside waiting for me."

"Tell her to come too. It's all good. The more the merrier," I replied.

"I'm sorry. Not tonight, but thank you, though." She shot me down. "You guys go have a good time. You deserve it."

I was a little disappointed, but was still on a spiritual and emotional high about what had just happened at the concert.

I thanked Alice for coming, she thanked me again for inviting her, and she turned and walked back down the aisle toward the back doors of the church. I watched her walk away. She was so beautiful! She looked back and smiled at me, and waved goodbye. I hated to see her leave, but loved watching her go. She went through the back doors, and walked off, out of my view. I headed to the after-party.

How in the world was I going to get a chance to spend more time with the woman that I believe was supposed to be my wife?

I knew that I had to find a way to spend time with Alice. My rationale was, "if she got to know me, she would love me." So, I needed to find a way to hang out with her. So one day, I gave her a call, and asked her what she liked to do in her spare time. She said she liked playing games, bowling, and things like that. Video games? Hmmm, how about challenging her to a game of Pac-man on campus?

I asked her if she'd like to hang out. She needed to run some errands in San Francisco, and asked me to join her. I met her at her apartment, and we walked back to the BART station, and sat on the concrete benches waiting for the train to come. All of sudden, I got nervous. I just could not relax for some reason. I was fidgety. I couldn't think of anything meaningful to say. She was so beautiful to me and I didn't want to blow it. It was very uncharacteristic of me to be nervous around women. I was "Manny Man!" on campus. The ladies loved me. The Football team gave me nicknames because I was so cool with all the beautiful women on campus. "So why in the world am I nervous?" I wondered. "This is not cool! Calm down, dude!"

Alice said something, and I couldn't even look at her for longer than a second before getting awkward. It was a shame! The more we walked, the more I was able to relax, but it was really embarrassing.

After running her errands, we went out to lunch at a chinese restaurant, and enjoyed more conversation. I was much more in my element by the middle of the day, and I began flirting innocently. I told her that I might go into politics one day, and she asked, "Manny, you gonna be president one day?"

I couldn't resist. I said, "I don't know, but you would make a great first lady." She just smiled in a dismissive kind of way.

We returned to her apartment, and I walked her to her door. In her apartment, I saw a picture of Alice and a group of people. It looked like her family. She had four brothers and a sister. She was the baby of six.

Next to that picture was a photo of her and some guy. They were hugging. It was obvious that it was the guy I had heard about from some people on campus. I washed my hands, and headed home.

I didn't even mention the picture. I acted like I didn't even see it. In her brain, she was relieved, because she thought that when I saw the picture, that I would know she had a boyfriend.

But that was his problem, not mine. She was supposed to be my wife. But I also knew that I only had a limited amount of time to reveal to Alice what my ultimate intentions were- to one day marry her. Every guy has a window of opportunity to let a woman know that he is interested. If he misses that window, he will forever be stuck into the "friend" zone, where she feels free to tell you about other guys she likes. In the friend zone, she tells you about problems she's having with other guys, and even starts asking you about some of your friends that she likes. If you miss your window, you become a brother or friend, forever. That's it. I was not going to let that window close without letting Alice know about what I believed our future could hold.

So I devised a plan. I had been listening to a lot of Stevie Wonder, and his song, "Overjoyed" was on repeat. That was my theme song during my season of pursuing Alice. I had to let Alice know that she was my "one." So I let my roommate know that I was going to drop off some flowers on her doorstep. We broke into her apartment building together, ran up the stairs, snuck toward her door, and I laid down a bouquet of a dozen roses. There was note inside. In that note, I let her know that I was seriously interested in being more than just her friend.

I left those flowers on a day I was scheduled to go to LA for a friend's wedding. I let a few days pass, and called Alice. She picked up, and she thanked me for the flowers. But I could tell she wanted to tell me about her boyfriend, so I dominated the conversation, then rushed off the phone before she could get it out.

I called a couple days later to see if she had come around, but she had the same tone. Not good. Again, I got off the phone quickly. It wasn't pretty, but it was all I had at the time.

About a week had passed before I returned to the Bay Area, and I knew I had to re-connect with Alice soon, to see where she was, and to get it off my chest. I had to tell her that she was supposed to be my wife.

One night, Aaron was out on a date with one of the most beautiful women on campus, Nicky Hogan. Jared went out on a date too. And there I was, at the house, not really wanting to hang out with anyone but Alice. Sure, I had options. But they were not really in my heart in the way Alice was.

So, I picked up the phone, and I figured, "I am going to feel her out, and see if she might want to hang out." She picked up the phone, and she sounded genuinely happy to hear from me. I told her about my trip home, and I intentionally did not bring up the flowers and note I left on her door the week before.

But I had to ask, "Alice, do you have a boyfriend?"

"Yeah," she said sheepishly.

I put it all on the line. "But God told me that you're supposed to be my wife."

"I have a boyfriend!"

"I know, you just told me that. But God told me that you're supposed to be my wife." That is not a line I recommend that anyone ever use. Ever. And yet, for me, it was true. In my soul, I was compelled to believe that she was my "one."

"But you don't even know me," she said.

"But I do. I feel like I've known you forever. And, God told me that you're supposed to be my wife. I know it sounds crazy, but it's true." I then explained my fast with Jon.

From the day at Clark Kerr and every moment since, my feelings for her only grew stronger. She then said, "My father said that God told him that my mom was supposed to be his wife too."

We talked for another hour or two, about life, about her relationship, and she told me that she knew she was not going to marry the guy she was with. That was ALL I needed to hear.

"Well, can we at least be friends?"

"Of course," she said.

I had to find a way to stay on her radar. "If she only gets to know me, she will love me." I just knew it.

Between that last conversation, about a month passed, and I made up reasons to call Alice. The little church I was attending at the time had bible studies in the middle of the week. After Bible study, I called Alice to see if I could come by. We hung out, we laughed, we talked, and had a wonderful connection.

During one of our calls, she invited me to drive down to L.A. with her and her cousin, Tricia. In the car, on our way down to LA, we connected in a very special way during our conversations. When she dropped me off, I tried to pay her for her gas, but she insisted that I should save it. "Maybe you can take me out to dinner when we return to the Bay." She had a deal!

She broke up with her boyfriend, and we returned to the Bay about a week later, and hung out more frequently. We eventually started dating, and went on to have the best college experience imaginable, enjoying our friendship, lunches, dinners, visiting book stores, and church together. We fell in love, and had one of the best seasons of our lives. Berkeley will always be dear to us because it is where our love was born and blossomed.

47

After I quit playing football, I spent more time reflecting on my identity and my journey. I had more time to think about who I wanted to become, since football or athletics were no longer in my future. It's always interesting how much your identity can be tied to your dreams or your position or title, and when you lose that dream, position, or title, you feel like you are losing a part of yourself. Who was I apart from football? Apart from my ability to catch a ball?

It was during that season of my life that I began to get more curious about who I was and where I came from. Those questions had always been rather difficult for me to answer. Am I a black man? Mixed? Am I a really a man, or is it possible that I missed the rite of passage into manhood and am I still functioning as a boy in a man's body?

With all this in mind, I thought it would be helpful to call my paternal grandmother, Betty Grate, to find answers.

I picked up the phone, dialed her number, and the phone rang. I hoped she picked up. She answered. Her high, somewhat squeaky voice said, "Hello?"

How should I identify myself to her. Should I say, "Yes, grandma, it's me." As Lito? No, she probably doesn't even know me by that name. "As Manuel Sarmiento, your grandson?" That might not help her either. "Your son's son?" I forgot what I said, but she knew who I was. I told her I was in college now, and learning a lot.

Then I jumped right into it. I asked her to tell me more about my father, my blood, my roots. She told me about her father, Francisco Poundeaux or Pointer, and that we were not descendants from Africa, but from some other black people. She said we were French Creole or something like that, and that he was a soldier, or something like that in the civil war, or some war. She said, "he's buried in Colorado."

I then asked her about my father's father. Who was he? What happened to him? I remember my father telling me that he only had vague memories of his father, sitting on his lap, and holding a steering wheel, but then he disappeared. So I figured he had died by now. Or, at least, was unfindable.

She told me his father's name was Roger Scott. I asked what happened to him. She told me that she had recently seen him in Amarillo at a senior citizens home. "The last time you saw him? He's still alive?" I asked Wow! All these questions flooded my mind: Why didn't my father know this? Why did my father think his father was dead? Why are you telling me more about my grandfather than my own father knows about him, and it's his dad? This is strange. All that raced through my mind.

I mentioned that I might call him, but she vehemently objected. She told me not to do that. To "please not do that. Oh, just leave them alone."

I became even more curious. Why was she so opposed to me finding out who I am, and who I'm from? I told her that I just wanted to look into it, and she angrily commanded me to not do that.

We wrapped things up, and I got off the phone. Her insistence that I not try to find my biological grandfather only made me more eager to find him. "Why was she so opposed to me finding him? What might she be keeping from me, and my father?" I wondered.

So I went on a mission. I needed to try to find my grandfather.

It was shortly after that conversation that I changed my name to Manuel Scott. It felt more befitting. It felt right.

During the days ahead, I spent time at the library, searching the internet for my roots. I searched for all of the people named Roger Scott in the state of Texas. About twenty names came up. I printed out the names, numbers and addresses of all of them, and rushed home to call them.

As soon as I got home, I called everyone on the list. The first person picked up, and I said, "Hello sir, my name is Manuel, and I am trying to find Roger Scott. He was the first black police officer of Gilmer, Texas. Do you know who he is?"

Time and time again, people said, "No sir, you have the wrong number."

I was near the bottom of the list, and I dialed the number, and someone picked up the phone.

"Hello?" The voice sounds just like my fathers, maybe a little older.

"Hello, yes, My name is Manuel Scott, and I am looking for Roger Scott, retired police chief, etc...."

"Well, he passed away, but I'm his son, Roger Scott Jr."

Wow! It was him! I was talking to my uncle. He sounded just like an older version of my father. I was in disbelief.

"Yes, well I think I am his grandson. My father's name is Raymond, and my father's mother's name is Betty Grate. Do you know who that is?"

There was a long pause, as though he was thinking, and then he responded, "Let me call you back."

I give him my number, and we hung up.

I was so excited. I found him. I found him! I felt great. I hoped he called me back. But I waited for several hours, really until about 11pm, and he still hadn't called. Then, at about 11:45pm, my phone rang, and I rushed to grab it.

It was him.

"Hello, Manuel?"

"Yes! I'm so glad you called back," I said

"Yes. Well, I wasn't going to call you back." He paused for a few seconds, then continued, "I know your grandmother. My family knows who she is, and my family doesn't really care too much about her. But I didn't think it was fair to hold that against you. That has nothing to do with you. You have a right to know who you are, so I called you back."

Why didn't they like my grandmother? I just listened while he kept talking. "You see son. My father and mother had seven kids. They had been married for a while, and my father had an affair with your grandmother. Your grandmother knew my mother, and knew daddy was married, and yet she would not leave daddy alone. Our mother committed suicide over the whole situation." There was a silence over the phone for several seconds.

Then went on, "So you see, son, my family was really hurt over that. And so we don't really have the greatest feelings about your grandmother."

I said, "I'm so sorry for your loss. I am terribly sorry for your loss."

He quickly responded, "But that has nothing to do with you, son. So I decided to call you back."

We talked for about fifteen or twenty more minutes, and we actually had a very nice conversation about the family. I told him about my father, and the challenges he faced throughout his life as a result of many factors. Near the end of our call, I asked him if I could call him every now and then.

"Please, call me uncle Roger. Son, I'm your uncle. Call me uncle Roger."

"Sounds good, Uncle Roger. Thank you for your call. It means so much to me."

I called my father as soon as I got off the phone, and told him the news. He was dumbfounded, and humbled that they wanted to meet him too. He felt, like me, an orphan who found his roots. He found out where he too had come from.

It was a very uplifting feeling. I was excited and felt like I knew a little more about myself, and who I was. It's hard to put that into words.

48

The day finally came. Standing on the stage at Berkeley's Hearst Greek Theater in my cap and gown, waiting to receive my degree, I looked out at the nearly 9,000 people who had come from all over the world to celebrate our graduation. They were dressed to impress in their Sunday's best. Like a vibrant Sunday service at a Black church, the entire audience in the theater became the choir, singing and praising, clapping, and swaying, uniting their spirits with the music that was blasting through the speakers:

"Take the shackles off my feet so I can dance.

I just wanna praise you, Just wanna praise you.

You broke the chains so I can lift my hands.

I just wanna praise you. I just wanna praise you."

We turned Berkeley, the paragon of protest, into the apotheosis of praise. All that gaiety and merriment was so full because many of our journeys had been so hard. Joy that has known no sorrow is no joy at all, for it is only through our deep and personal intimacy with great grief that our hearts can fully experience great joy.

My joy, like a cup overflowing, was quite replete. Standing there, a hurricane of emotions stirred in my soul. Breathing hard upon my remembrance were all the doubts and discouragements, all the dejection and despair, and all the homeless shelters, and all the dumpsters, and all the alcohol, and all the drugs, and all the fights, and all the abuse, and all the blood, and all the death, and all the pain, and all the tears that I endured.

Then they called my name.

I walked proudly across the stage, and received my degree, becoming the first person in my family to graduate from college. I'd been through so much in my life, but I made it! I should have been addicted to drugs, but I made it! I should have been locked up, but I made it! I should have been dead, but I made it! I made it through the dark days. I made it through the starless nights. I made it!

After they handed me my degree, I looked out at the sea of celebration, so I could really take in the fullness of the moment. While looking out, I saw her face. I wasn't sure she was going to be able to make it, but she did. It was momma. She was sitting by herself between two well-dressed families who looked like they had been to a few college graduations. Unable to contain her emotion, tears began rolling down momma's face. Dabbing her tears with a piece of tissue, she mouthed, "I love you."

As soon as the ceremony was over, I jumped off the stage, ran to her, and gave her the biggest hug. Without really saying too much, we just hugged each other, because we both knew just how much that day meant to us.

49

That summer after graduation, a friend of mine asked me to be a part of Cal Camp, a week-long camp dedicated to sponsoring as many as 100 youth who were a part of social services system. Many of them lived in foster homes, were orphans, and had been neglected and abused.

In addition to hiking, swimming, and a plethora of other fun activities, I taught daily workshops on goal-setting, self-respect, moral and academic excellence. I kept it very real with the young people, hoping to steer some of them clear of crime, drugs, and mediocrity.

During my week, I spent a lot of time with the young people, listening to them, getting to know them. One night, at a campfire, a young girl, about ten years old, told me about how several of her male family members had raped her; and, as a result of the damage they inflicted on her uterus, she would never be able to have babies.

Another young man told me about how his father was locked up, and that he had been pretty much on his own, raising himself. Although he was still a little boy, he had the numbness and maturity of someone much older. Pain has a way of growing you up.

That week, I sat with the kids, laughing with them, and enjoying my time with them. The more time I spent with them, the more I saw younger versions of myself. Some of them had holes in their shoes. Some had hand-me-down clothes. Some had shoes that were too big, too old, and clothes that didn't fit. Yet, in their eyes and hearts, they, like the younger me, had dreams too. They too had hopes. They, like me, just wanted to be somebody. They wanted to matter. They wanted to feel safe. They wanted someone to understand them, connect with them, and believe in them. They wanted to be loved.

And yet they were so hardened by life, by the challenges that lived with them day by day.

The last night of the camp, all the counselors and kids were sitting around a big campfire. The kids and counselors got up to say what they enjoyed most about the experience, and what they were going to take away from the week. Although all of the children would, in less than 24 hours, be returning to environments that were very broken and dysfunctional, many of the words of encouragement being offered by some the other counselors were, at best, superficial. Not because they were callous and insensitive, I hope. Rather, I think their comments really came from their middle and upper-class backgrounds, which were very different from the penury that most of those young people lived with every day of their lives.

Sitting there, I knew that something more substantive needed to be said, but did not think that I would be the person to say it. But as the night's end drew near, and the profusion of empty, meaningless clichés poured fourth, I started getting more and more restless.

My heart was racing, and then a strange, yet familiar feeling came over me. It was the same feeling I had when I was crying in my room after that woman put out a cigarette on my face when I was seven years old; it was the same feeling I had on that park bench when Martin Stevens talked to me; and, it was the same feeling I had when I was fasting and felt the conviction that Alice was supposed to one day be my wife. It was that same feeling, that tugging, that burning, that I had been running from throughout college. That feeling returned and rested on me that night at the campfire. It's presence was undeniable; it's power was irresistible. I could not talk myself out of it. I could not explain it away. It was really like a fire flaming in my bones.

I knew then that Someone greater than me was pushing me to speak, to say something to those kids. However, the enormity of that task towered over me, and mocked my shortcomings as a speaker. I did not consider myself to be a good speaker. Sure, I had hosted some campus shows, and encouraged kids during some workshops on campus. But that was different. Very different. "But what if I fail? What if everyone laughs at me? What if…?" I asked. "Who am I, and what could I possibly say to these kids that will make any lasting difference in their lives?"

But in that clutch of self-doubt, it seemed as though God spoke directly to my heart, "My son, who better than you? I brought you out of the same conditions these kids are being raised in. I delivered you from homelessness and hunger, from an abusive alcoholic, addicted home. I brought you out of the misery and the depression that these kids know very well. I brought you out of the pain, I brought you out…So, who better than you to give these kids hope? Who better than you to encourage them? Who better than you to tell them they can make it?"

So I rose to speak, with a quivering voice, and shaky knees. I opened my mouth, and the words just began to flow. I began to tell the kids in essence, "I have had a great time with you guys this week. I loved listening to your stories, and getting to know you. I thank you for sharing your lives with me. I will never, ever forget you.

"Tonight is our last night together. Tomorrow we all go home. Some of us are going to go on to become doctors and lawyers and do some great things in the world, and some people are going to back to some very difficult places. Some of you here are going to be going back to places that are hard on you. Some of you are going to be going back to places where you don't feel loved. Some of you are going back to places where you are going to feel very alone."

Tears began to fall from my eyes. "I've been there. I've spent many nights crying myself to sleep. I've spent many nights feeling alone and hopeless, and I want you to know that when you get to those places, and you feel alone; when you feel discouraged, I want you to know that you are not alone. I want you to know that there is a God who loves you, who knows all about what you're going through. And I want you to know that you can make it through the pain. You can make it through the brokenness. You can make it through the sadness. You can make it through the night. So don't you give up!"

"I've been there, many, many nights, and I want you to know that you can break the cycle of misery in your family. You can have a good life. Things can get better for you. You can be the first person in your family to graduate from high school. You can be the first person in your family to graduate from college. You can become the man you never met. You can one day be the kind of father you never had. One day you can be the kind of momma you have always wanted. You can have a happy, healthy family. You can have a life so good that you don't have to worry, or watch your back, or cry yourself to sleep anymore. So don't give up!"

"But it is going to take some hard work. It is going to take you making up your mind. It is going to take you fighting for what you want out of life. Yes, you might get tired sometimes, but don't you stop fighting for a better life. Don't you ever stop believing things can get better. Don't you ever give up! Don't you ever throw in the towel..."

By the time I was finished speaking, there wasn't a dry eye around that campfire. I was inspired that night, and the experience was so powerful, so unforgettable, that I realized, that night, that I had a very important decision to make about my future.

50

Shortly after I descended from that mountaintop at Cal Camp, I found a job at a prestigious law firm in San Francisco. I was hired as a file clerk. Initially, I was excited by the opportunity because I believed it would prepare me for law school. In reality, however, I quickly discovered my title was merely a sophisticated name for flunky. Really, a high school graduate, barely able to alphabetize, could have done that job. While that job may have been fine for someone else, it was frustrating for me.

My office was even more disappointing. It was not even fair to call what I had an office. It was really a small, windowless file room, with dimmed, florescent lights that hurt your eyes if you stayed in there for too long. Along the walls were shelves that stretched, like prison bars, to the ceiling. In the middle of the room sat two rectangular tables, which were stacked with boxes that were stuffed with files. There was a desk in the corner, but that belonged to my supervisor, and it was the only place in that dungeon that was not covered with boxes or shelves. I didn't have a desk; I just had a chair that I slid around the room as needed.

My supervisor, Pablo Santiago was a short, stocky guy whose family was from South America. He was balding, wore rayon shirts, raggedy blue jeans and tennis shoes to work every day. He hardly ever shaved, and never, ever wore a tie. He looked like the kind of guy the mob would hire to do some of its dirty work. Pablo had me do both my work and his, but since I was paying my dues, I didn't mind the extra work, initially.

However, shortly after I started working there, I noticed Perry was prone to disappear for long periods of time. He would tell me he had to go to the basement to locate files, but I suspected that there was more to the story. So one day I decided to go see where Perry was really going. I took the elevator down to the basement of the building, and walked into a big, dark, warehouse-looking room filled with thousands of boxes that were stacked high and wide, from wall to wall. Like a private investigator, I snuck into the dusty room, and quietly scanned. I didn't see Pablo, but I heard something. It sounded like heavy breathing. Sure enough, when I tipped toward the sound, and looked around the corner, there he was, sleeping in between some boxes!

That was my job. I showed up, filed documents and folders, talked to almost no one, then left, every day. It was the most boring and demeaning job in the firm- not because the work itself was insignificant (because all work has dignity), but because of the way everyone in the office treated us. When I tried to talk with some of the attorneys about my ambitions to become a lawyer, their apathy could not have been more appalling. While cordial, most of them showed no interest in showing me the ropes.

After several months, I grew to hate the job. It became harder and harder for me to show up. I thought to myself, "I have a college education from one of the finest schools in the world, and I am filing papers in a dead-end job." While I have a tremendous amount of respect for those who, in order to provide their families, do that kind of work for a lifetime, I could not see myself as a file clerk for another day.

So when I shared my concerns that I was being underutilized, and wanted to do more, the office manager generously allowed me to also file the newspapers in the daily newspaper rack. I wondered to myself, "I asked to do more, and you give me newspapers to file? Ok, I see where this is going." I took the job hoping I would learn about the law, and learn some things that could help me prepare for law school. However, the only thing I learned at that firm is you can't always wait for other people to promote you. If you want something, you have to go get it. You have to believe in yourself, and take risks on yourself, and reach for more. So, without another job lined up, I quit. To scare me into staying, the office manager warned me that the legal community in San Francisco is close-knit, and said that I would not be able to find work at any other firms.

She was wrong. A month later, I found a job at another big-name law firm that paid a lot more money and gave me more respect and responsibility. They hired me as a Litigation Specialist, and gave me my own office, with one of the nicest views of the San Francisco Bay. My new situation was lovely.

After years of hard work, and countless hours in libraries, and pulling all-nighters, I was finally able to support myself for the first time in my life. My hard work paid off. The extra money enabled me to eat at nice restaurants, and buy nice things for myself and others. It allowed me to buy a car, and to lease a little studio apartment in Oakland, California.

However, the glamour of that firm soon wore off too. No matter how much money I made, or how hard I tried, I could not find fulfillment in the work I was doing at the law firm. While I had a passion for justice, I just couldn't see myself as a lawyer. I could not see myself working in that kind of environment for the rest of my life. I couldn't see myself playing petty office-politics, and giving my entire life to things that I didn't really feel passionate about or enjoy. So, after the allure of making good money wore off, my work at the firm lost its significance, and I began to think more and more about finding a way to do something that fulfilled me.

I searched my soul to discover the purpose of my life. Why was I put on this earth? What am I supposed to do before I breath my final breath? My mind and heart went back to my experience at Cal Camp. That was it! I am supposed to help people. I was created to help people. To serve people. To empower people. To give them hope.

I thought that maybe I could become a speaker, and try to help others, and lovingly serve them. I felt a passion to help the least, the last, the lost, and the left out. I felt a burden to help those who were in need of hope. I felt compelled to help people who were living beneath their potential by inspiring them, and empowering them, to reach for, and achieve more.

So I had to make decision- was I going to stay in my nice, cushy, safe job, making pretty good money, which exposed me to the finer things in life? Or, was I going to go with my gut, and risk being completely broke? Was I going to really trust the burden weighing heavy on my heart- the deep conviction that there was more for me to do with my life? Was I going to believe that somehow the dreams that I had been getting in my sleep- dreams of me speaking to large numbers of people; visions of me traveling the world giving people hope and practical help- was I going to just let those dreams die, or was I going to believe that those dreams were supposed to somehow come true? Was I going to give my life to making a living, or give my life to making a difference? At the time I did not believe it was possible to do both.

So one night, that internal battle, between money and service, between helping myself or helping others. became so intense that I could not sleep. I was struggling in my head and heart, wondering, "If I don't surrender to this burden, this vision, this calling, this passion, this magnificent obsession, what will happen to all those people out there who need my help? What will happen to all of those people who need to hear me speak? What will happen to all the people who are about to give up? If I don't speak, where will they end up? How many more young men will go to prison? How many more parents will have to bury their sons? How many more girls will have to raise their children alone? How many more youth will quit school and begin selling drugs? How many families will never find healing, if I don't give my life to helping them?"

I concluded, "I may not make a lot of money, and I may never make a name for myself; I may never have fine and luxurious things; but, at least I will have lived for something bigger than myself. At least I will have been true to this calling that I'm feeling. At least I will have been true to myself. At least I will have tried. If I have nothing to lose by trying, and everything to gain by trying, then I must at least try."

I did not want to keep rolling in bed all night, battling my conscience. I couldn't keep going through the motions like so many people around me were doing, and act like there was not a burden on my heart or a calling on my life.

So I submitted my letter of resignation, and stepped out, in faith, into the unknown. I didn't know what the future would hold, but I believed I knew who held my future. In faith, I made the decision that I was going to face my fears and fight for my future. I made a decision to become a speaker, a messenger of hope, a catalyst for change, a page turner. I made a decision to give my life to love, to serve, to help, to reach, to teach, to preach, and to save people. I made a decision to live for things that will have eternal significance. That decision has made all the difference in my life.

Afterword

I have shared parts of my story with you not to impress you, but to impress upon your head and heart some important lessons.

First, I hope that you have seen that no matter where you are in your story, it is never too late for you to turn the page. It is never too late for you to turn things around, to start anew, to begin afresh. I hope you see that, like me, you too can write new chapters in your life. You too can write new chapters filled with hope, and healing, and perseverance and possibility. You too can take responsibility for your life, and begin creating the kind of life that you really want. I hope that you get clear about the quality of life you would like to have. Get clear about the kind of person you would like to become. Get clear about the kinds of things you would like to do. Get clear about the kinds of things you would like to learn. Get clear about the kinds of places you would like to go. Get clear about the kinds of things you would like to do for others. Get clear about what you really want out of life. Then, get clear about what's in your way that might be keeping you from achieving those dreams.

I also hope, through your time with my book, that you have seen the power of decision. We are all a product of our environments, our genetics, and our choices. Of those three factors, our personal decisions, our choices, are the most powerful thing we have. You have the power to make decisions that can change the quality of your life forever. No matter where you are from, no matter how much schooling you have (or don't have), no matter what you were before this moment, you have the power to make a decision to turn everything around.

Making a decision to change your life does not have to take years or decades. Your life can change immediately. Let me explain. When you make a decision, you commit and then you cut. You commit to achieving a specific goal, and then you cut yourself off from any other possibility. When you truly decide, action flows from those decisions. When you truly make a decision, something begins to change in that moment, because you have taken action. To be sure, to manage those decisions, and follow-through on them, takes time and hard work. But when you think about the long-term benefits of those decisions, the temporary sacrifices and discomforts become worth it. So what kind of decisions to you need to make in your life right now? What is one thing you can decide right now that could have the greatest impact on the overall quality of your life? Whatever your situation in life is right now, I hope that you have seen that you have a power that is greater than your conditions. You have a power that is greater than your environment. Yes, greater than your problems is your power to decide. Your decisions, more than your difficulties, shape the ultimate quality of your life every day.

In addition to seeing the power of decision, I hope you have come to appreciate the power of your beliefs. If you are going to achieve your dreams, if you are going to make any significant changes in your life, that you have to make sure that you have the right beliefs in your head and in your heart. What do I mean? I believe that your future depends on your actions, and that your actions depend on your decisions. I believe that your beliefs determine the kinds of decisions we make. So if you don't believe that you need to make any changes in your life, then you probably won't. If you believe that everything in your life is fine right now, then you won't decide to change anything. If you don't believe that people like you can achieve your wildest dreams, then you will never get around to deciding to chase those dreams. You see, your beliefs can hold you back, or they can build you up. Your beliefs can position you for failure, or they can catapult you to success. You beliefs are foundational to everything we think and feel and do in life. So, you have to get to the place where you actually believe that you can change. You have to believe that you must change. You have to believe that your future can be better than your past. You have to believe that you are greater than your circumstances. You have to believe that you not a victim, but a survivor. You have to believe that you are smart enough, you are strong enough, that you have what it take to change your situation, and change your environment, and change your life. You have to believe. You have to have faith. You have to have the confidence that things can and will get better, and that you have the power to make it so. My friend, it is your faith, and your beliefs, that helps you make it through the tough times. It is your faith that empowers you achieve that dream or that goal. It is your faith that allows you feel in your head and heart that which you cannot yet touch with your hands. If you have any beliefs that are in the way of you becoming the person you were created to be, then you must confront those head on. You most evict those beliefs from your head and heart, and replace them with more powerful, productive ones.

Furthermore, I hope all those dreams, decisions, and beliefs lead you to take action! Take action today by eliminate anything in your life, any limiting beliefs, any negative influences, that are holding you back. Take action today and every day to get yourself one step closer to your dreams. You have to have a whole lot of little successes, so they can lead you to your big success. One of the biggest secrets of getting ahead is getting started. So get started today, and work toward making your dreams a part of your everyday reality.

In addition to seeing things that can help you improve your own life, I also hope that you see the power of love. I am who I am, and where I am, today not only because I have done things to improve my life. I am also here today largely because several people came into my life and helped me. With hearts filled with love, and souls generated by grace, many others have sacrificed their own personal comforts in order to make a difference in my life. I seriously doubt that I would be where I am in my life right now if it had not been for a man who met me on a park bench; or a teacher who believed in me; or coaches who pushed me; or secretaries, janitors, lunch ladies, librarians, and many other people who went out of their way to encourage me, support me, confront me, and love me.

My life is the product of the love and sacrifice of many unsung heroes who may never have a movie made about them. People who work in the obscurity of everyday life to make a difference in the lives of others. They have given their time and their resources to give people hope and practical help. They live with a burden to not only make a living but, more importantly, to make a difference. They may never be rich financially, and may never acquire some of the fine and luxurious material things in life, or have their names appear in lights. Nonetheless, they are the true heroes of the world. They deserve to be praised. For the well-being of others they sacrifice themselves. They are soldiers. They are teachers, counselors, librarians, and nurses; they are superintendents, board members, principals and coaches; they are bus drivers, janitors, cafeteria-workers, and volunteers. They are the true heroes and she roes of the world, for they are the people, who, despite their own challenges, sacrifice themselves to make our world a better, more beautiful place. For them, I am so thankful. I am thankful to have been touched by their kindness and love. I am grateful to have been blessed by each and every one of them.

Therefore, I hope you see that you too, no matter what you are doing with your life, have the power to make a difference in the life of someone else. I hope you see that who you are, right now, is enough- enough to change a life, enough to give someone hope, and enough to give someone help. Right now, against, all odds, you have the power to impact someone's life. On your worst day, you might be their best hope. On your worst day, you might be their last chance.

So live for something bigger than yourself. You have the power to help them. You have the power to help them turn the page, and write new chapters in their lives. You have the power to help them see that things can get better. You have the power to help them see that they are loved, that they matter, that they are here for a reason. You, my friend, have the power to make this world a better place. You have the power to change the world, one word, one act of kindness, one gesture of love, at a time.

So, keep writing, and keep using your power to create a better life; and, keep working to make this world a better place- a place where people are no longer homeless; a place where people are no longer hungry; a place where the least, the last, the lost, and the left out of our world are loved. Please- I beg you. Love, work, and serve others like your life depends on it, because someone else's life probably does. Turn the Page! Write Now!

About the Author

An original Freedom Writer whose story is told in part in the 2007 hit movie, Freedom Writers, Manny Scott has energized over a million leaders, educators, volunteers, and students worldwide with his authentic, inspiring messages of hope. As the founder and CEO of Ink International, Manny Scott has spoken for the past fourteen years to hundreds of groups a year. He is the speaker of choice for conferences, conventions, schools, fundraisers, and banquets.

He is happily married to Alice, and they have three children. He is a successful entrepreneur, a PhD student, and one of the nation's most sought after speakers.

For more info and resources to help you turn the page, contact us at:

Ink International

P.O. Box 464868

Lawrenceville, GA 30042

Phone: (888) 987-TURN

Or visit our website at:

www.MannyScott.com

39027096R00151

Made in the USA
Middletown, DE
02 January 2017